THE SENSATIONAL TRIAL . . .
THE DEVASTATING
PERSONAL STORY!

For the first time in legal history, a woman sues her psychiatrist for sexual malpractice—AND WINS!

Betrayal

The day-by-day court drama of that scandalous trial is "inspiring, moving, a real page-turner . . . Julie Roy's remarkable suit against her psychiatrist is a great step forward for all women."
—Barbara Seaman

"The case of *Roy v. Hartogs* was a landmark decision on twentieth-century morality; its impact ranks with that of the 1934 decision allowing the publication of James Joyce's *Ulysses* in this country. *Betrayal* is the story behind the case, told in moving and dramatic terms by the woman who brought the suit. The book is important reading for lawyers, for doctors, for anyone attuned to the times."
—Morris L. Ernst, Esq.,
defense attorney in the *Ulysses* case

LUCY FREEMAN and JULIE ROY

Betrayal

The True Story of the First
Woman to Successfully Sue Her
Psychiatrist for Using Sex in the
Guise of Therapy

A KANGAROO BOOK
PUBLISHED BY POCKET BOOKS NEW YORK

BETRAYAL

Stein and Day edition published 1976

POCKET BOOK edition published February, 1977

This POCKET BOOK edition includes every word contained in
the original, higher-priced edition. It is printed from brand-
new plates made from completely reset, clear, easy-to-read type.
POCKET BOOK editions are published by
POCKET BOOKS,
a division of Simon & Schuster, Inc.,
A GULF+WESTERN COMPANY
630 Fifth Avenue,
New York, N.Y. 10020.
Trademarks registered in the United States
and other countries.

ISBN: 0-671-81042-1.
Library of Congress Catalog Card Number: 75-37965.
Front cover photograph by Terry McKee.
Back cover photograph, *New York Daily News* Photo.

Printed in the U.S.A.

to Bob and Loren,
with deepest thanks

This book is based on an actual trial—a successful legal action taken by a woman patient against a psychiatrist on the ground that she had been advised to enter into a sexual relationship with him as a part of "therapy." The trial in the case of Roy v. Hartogs took place in the Civil Court of New York County, beginning March 10, 1975. The jury handed down a verdict in favor of the patient on March 19, 1975. The doctor appealed to the Appellate Term, but on January 30, 1976, the verdict for the plaintiff was affirmed.

Every effort has been made to give an accurate report of the proceedings and of the events described in the course of the trial. The entire account is true, but some names have been changed.

The authors thank Sheila Moran of the *New York Post* for providing additional sidelights on the trial, Robert Stephan Cohen and Loren H. Plotkin for their support and assistance, Sol Stein and Ken Giniger for seeing the value of the book for the psychic freedom of troubled men and women, and Michaela Hamilton for helping to shape the book in content and style.

JULIE ROY
LUCY FREEMAN

... Whatever houses I may visit, I will come for the benefit of the sick, remaining free of all intentional injustice, of all mischief and, in particular, of sexual relations with both female and male persons, be they free or slave.

—The Hippocratic Oath

1

Julie Roy sat waiting, her eyes fixed on the door through which the judge would enter the courtroom. Today—Monday, March 10, 1975—she would take the witness stand to give testimony against a man she had once considered only slightly less than a god.

Though she was the plaintiff in the case of *Roy* v. *Hartogs,* she felt she would be the one on trial: She would be tested, her veracity questioned, her personal life revealed to the court and to the world.

Her two attorneys, Bob Cohen and Loren Plotkin, sat at the counsel table in front of her, along with the two lawyers for the defense. She looked at them over a guard rail that separated the spectators' section, where she sat, from the legal arena.

She knew Bob and Loren were as tense as she. Four years ago they had taken on her suit because they believed in its importance for legal history, and because they wanted to right what Bob called "a terrible injustice." In a few days she would be either vindicated or disgraced.

She looked around the small, modern courtroom, Room 621 of the Civil Court of the County of New York at 111 Centre Street. Bob had argued his first law school case here. In front of her, to the left, stood the jury box; to the right, a desk and chair for the court officer and a second chair for the judge's law secretary.

A sign above the judge's bench read, "In God We Trust."

She lowered her eyes to the judge's desk, then looked left, one step down, to the chair she would occupy as witness. She shivered, imagining the disapproval of her mother, who used to punish her for calling attention to herself in front of company—"displaying herself," her mother called it.

When the lawsuit was first announced, the television networks and the Associated Press had flashed the news coast to coast and overseas: A woman was suing her former psychiatrist for an unheard-of $1,250,000 in malpractice damages on the grounds he induced her to have sex with him as part of therapy.

The trial itself no doubt would make headlines too, for there had never been another like it. Sitting in the front row, directly across the aisle from Julie, was Sheila Moran of the *New York Post,* the only reporter yet to appear. Julie smiled shyly at young, dark-haired Sheila and felt happy to have her company.

Now she was being called to the witness stand.

Luckily for her, she thought, the man against whom she was bringing the suit was not in the courtroom. Only his lawyers knew whether Dr. Renatus Hartogs would appear at all. Julie half hoped he would stay away, at least until she completed her testimony.

As she rose from her seat, she felt stiff, as though her limbs had hardened to keep her from falling to pieces. She gained courage from the realization that she could rely on Bob to guide her with his questions and weave a strong web of truth from her answers.

She walked through the swinging gate and approached the judge and jury. Her long, light-brown hair was

parted in the middle and caught at the back with a bar-
rette. She wore no lipstick, just a touch of makeup. She
had taken off her plum-colored mohair cape, one she
had made, uncovering a navy sweater and ankle-length
skirt of navy and plum print, which she had also made.

She raised her right hand, placed her left hand on the
Bible, and promised "to tell the truth, the whole truth,
and nothing but the truth." After she climbed the few
steps to sit in the witness chair, Bob Cohen began the
questioning.

"Julie, would you tell the court, please, and the jury,
your age and where you were born?" he asked.

"I am thirty-six years old," she said. "I was born in
Port Huron, Michigan."

Cohen said, "Please raise your voice so the last juror,"
the one furthest from her, "and I can hear you." Then
he went on: "Tell us about your schooling, please."

"I finished high school in Port Huron, Michigan. I
have twelve years of schooling, no college," she said.
Though she tried to speak distinctly, her voice was soft
and low.

Samuel Halpern, the chief attorney for the defense,
interrupted her. "Your Honor, it is just a waste of time.
I can't hear her," he said.

Judge Allen Murray Myers said to her from his bench,
"You are going to have to try to shout."

*Keep still, Julie. Don't be a nuisance. Don't bother
people with your chatter.*

When she was little, the best thing she could be was
quiet. And twenty-five years later she still thought being
quiet was an essential part of being "good." Her mother
had tried hard to do what was right for her children. She

kept telling them she was "doing her duty" by them, reminding them *she* never would leave them as their father had done.

Her mother had married when she finished high school and spent the rest of her life raising four children and keeping her home clean and "respectable." She brought up her children to be "moral," to aim at bettering themselves in life.

She was a distant, reserved woman. When her husband left home, she had become even more withdrawn. Had she not been a strict Catholic, she might have gone out with other men after the divorce. But she refused all requests for dates and showed no interest in the possibility of ever marrying again, though she hoped her daughters would make good matches.

Julie's mother's parents were Irish; her father's mother was Swedish, his father French. She recalled some vague tragedy about her father's early life; he had lost either his mother or both parents when he was a child. He had some relatives, for they invited her one summer to visit them, but her mother would not hear of it.

Julie once asked her mother, "Why did you marry my father?"

"Because I felt sorry for him," her mother said. Then she added, "And to get away from my family."

At least her mother had been honest. But Julie suspected this loveless marriage had been a destructive factor in the lives of all of them.

She had felt depressed ever since she could remember; she had always thought of herself as bad, ugly, unwanted. She felt nothing she did merited praise. She believed feeling low was part of living, that she could never do anything about it, that the feeling would only get more and more intense until it finally destroyed her.

But she finally managed a move in her own behalf. Away from home, away from her mother, she made up her mind to see a psychiatrist in the hope of overcoming the depression that had gripped her all her life.

And now the judge was telling her to speak louder. Bob and Loren had worked so long to give her this chance. It was terribly important for people to hear her. She would speak as loudly as she could.

Julie Roy said once again, "I had twelve years of schooling. I finished high school in Port Huron, Michigan. . . ."

She was sure she was the dullard of the century. Some children did well in grade school but became dunces in high school; some did poorly in grade school, then blossomed in high school. But she was thickheaded from kindergarten on.

Directions confused her. If a teacher said, "Turn to page eight," she could not find it. She could not even get into the right line when the teacher said, "Boys on the left, girls on the right."

It wasn't that she was good in some subjects but poor in others; she failed in everything. When she was in seventh grade, her teachers gave her a series of tests to determine whether she should be put in a school for retarded children, but the test showed she had a very high I.Q. No one could explain why she could not learn.

Because she could never seem to gather all her thoughts in one place, her mind would not retain facts.

She made a heroic effort to learn the multiplication tables, but still had trouble remembering the sevens and nines. She could not do school assignments, either writing papers or working arithmetic problems. She never knew the answers to questions asked in class. She remembered an algebra test where she could not answer one question, started to cry, and had to leave the room. She would never dream of playing truant—her mother had told her to go to school, so she went—but she suffered every second she was there.

Once she tried to think for herself—in seventh grade, when she attended a Catholic school. A priest conducted one class a week in religion, and she disagreed with some of his teachings. She thought "sin" had a place on earth; that if God, who was omnipotent, created the devil Lucifer, then Lucifer had a rightful place in the world. When she told this to the priest, he looked at her in horror, the other children laughed, and she was sent into the hall as punishment.

She told her mother she thought banishing Adam and Eve from the Garden of Eden for taking a bite of an apple was unfair punishment. She asked why, if the Garden of Eden was such a paradise, a snake was allowed there. She said she was going to ask the priest this.

"You'll make a fool of yourself," her mother warned. "Don't you say a word to the priest." And she didn't.

She must have attended at least fourteen schools, including summer schools, because they moved so often. They went to Florida for a while to live with her mother's sister, then to Muskegon, Michigan, where her mother's mother lived, while they rented out their house in Port Huron. When they returned, they had to live in another house until the rental lease on their own expired, and that meant another school district.

Twice she was sent away from home to Catholic boarding schools. One of the schools was in Maine, the other in Michigan. She loathed them both, and got such poor grades that neither would keep her longer than one year. The nuns were strict, forbidding any show of intimacy by the girls, even holding hands.

She had no sense of permanent roots. Maybe, she thought, her fear of unfamiliar places stemmed from all that moving around in her early years. Perhaps if we don't have something we need when we are little, we will always be looking for it when we grow up.

Sometimes she wondered if she did so poorly in school because she used up all her energy in worrying about such questions as who she might have lunch with, whether anyone would walk home with her after school, who would be her friend that day. If pupils had been graded on social skills, she would have received failing marks there too.

Her physical development had always been slow. Her mother said she did not learn to sit up when most babies did; her mother would try to prop her up and she would collapse as though she had no bones, as she did now when she was depressed. When she was five, she did not have as much hair as other little girls, though it later grew in thick. She could not remember envying boys or wishing to be a boy, though when she moved to Manhattan she thought it preferable to be a man, because if she took a walk at night she was hailed as a hooker.

* * *

Cohen was asking, "Julie, can you tell me, please, about your family?"

"My parents were divorced when I was three years old," she said. "I was the youngest of four children. . . ."

Before their father left, they had lived in a two-story house. When she was seven, they moved to a one-story home in a somewhat rural area. Her mother loved plants, grew them in window boxes. The living room was cozy and rustic. In the center stood the Franklin stove, which had arrived, crated, one exciting day from Portland, Maine, and had to be installed ceremoniously in its setting of natural bricks. The kitchen was large and doubled as sitting room, complete with rocking chair. Its large picture window looked out on trees and wild shrubbery. There was also a large screened-in porch, which they used as a living room in summer.

Her mother, who was only four feet, eleven inches tall, was of average weight for her height, with blue eyes and brown hair that she always kept well groomed, and upswept. Julie thought she resembled her mother in coloring and facial features. Her father, whose nickname was "Shorty," was five feet, four inches. He had been a very thin man, she recalled.

As a child, she had preferred her sister Janey, twelve years older, because she was the most generous, giving of herself and the money she earned when she left high school for a while to help support the family. Allan, who was eight years older than Julie, had blond hair and blue eyes and reminded her of Peter O'Toole.

Carol, ten years older than Julie, wrote poetry and played the piano. By the time Carol was sixteen, she was part of a wild crowd at school. Julie remembered how she and her mother would often wait up, sometimes until four in the morning, for Carol to come home. Her mother would cry and say to Julie, "Promise me you will never make me as unhappy as Carol is making me." Julie promised.

None of the older children had gone to college, either, though they were all intelligent—probably, she thought, because they were enmeshed too tightly in the chaos created by their parents' separation.

From the day her father left, her mother cried a lot. Julie remembered a time when she was about six and shopping with her mother in a drugstore. Her mother met a woman she knew, started to talk about her husband, and burst into tears. Julie was so embarrassed she crawled in back of the counter.

The rest of the mothers on the block would stand around and talk as their children played together on the street, but her mother never joined them. Her mother would say contemptuously, "They're probably talking about me." Julie thought her mother was imagining this, but when she was older she realized the other mothers probably *were* talking about hers. Thirty years ago in a small town it was strange for a husband to walk out on a wife and four children. She didn't remember any other child whose parents were divorced or even separated.

Her mother played bridge occasionally with friends, and held a few brief jobs, once in an office, once in a department store. But she didn't feel she should work because, she said, "Julie has to be taken care of." Julie grew up hearing the family say they wanted to go here or there "but what are we going to do with Julie?"

Sometimes they made arrangements for other mothers to take care of her (her mother would never trust her to a baby-sitter). On the one hand, Julie had felt like a precious China doll; on the other, a nuisance to be gotten out of the way.

Her mother had two living sisters; Julie had been named for a younger one, who had died in childhood. Julie thought there was something depressing about being named for a dead person. Her mother sometimes quarreled with one sister or the other, but instead of releasing their anger in a blowup, they would cut each other off and not talk for months. Her mother had been raised to bear her problems and disappointments in silence. Had her husband not asked for a divorce, she would have stayed with him and suffered without complaining until she died.

The children all left home as soon as they were old enough. Janey got married, so did Carol, and Allan left the moment the Navy would take him. They all fled, though they never really got away, she thought. They stayed just as concerned about what their mother thought as they had been as children.

Carol's reaction was one of passive rebellion. Janey left home to marry a man her mother disapproved of. At the start of World War II, Janey had gotten a job as a checker in the A&P. A woman customer had a son overseas in the Army who was lonely, and Janey began corresponding with him. When he came home he proposed.

When Janey told her mother she was going to marry Angus, her mother said, "You can't! He's wrong for you." That was all she had to say. If she had said, "He's probably a very nice man but think about it for a while," Janey might have waited, learned to know him better. They were not a very well-matched couple. Janey loved to read, Angus loved hunting, fishing, the outdoors.

After her marriage and the first few babies, Janey seemed to want to sleep all the time. When she wasn't sleeping she was reading, and disorder piled up around her. She had no routine for cooking, shopping, or cleaning. Every so often she would show a flurry of activity, clean the house, make a delicious meal, then sink back into lethargy the next day. Janey's marriage and the way she lived seemed wholesale rebellion against the way she was brought up by her obsessively orderly mother, who would not allow her daughters to cook in the kitchen unless they tied their hair back so no stray hair would fall into the food.

Julie had liked Angus. He brought her balloons when when he was courting Janey. He seemed a simple man, clever with his hands. He built the house Janey and he lived in. He probably should have married someone else, but having had five children, he and Janey did their best to make the marriage work.

While growing up, Julie did not feel close to any member of her family. Though she spent time at Janey's home, she was too much a child at ten and eleven to take pleasure in Janey's first children. She did not like being displaced as the child in the family, and she resented the attention her mother gave to the new babies. Besides, instead of being taken care of herself, she now had to baby-sit when she was "told," not "asked."

But despite her resentment, she always did what her mother ordered. Rebellion was unthinkable. She sometimes thought back on herself, a child who never uttered one defiant word, and wondered: Had she ever been an active, precocious child? Had she at one time shown a lot of spirit, which her mother had to tame to suit her preconceptions of what a little girl should be? Could this taming have happened so early in her life that now all she could remember was being the submissive, obedient child her mother wanted?

She remembered one day when her mother dressed her in white socks, white shoes, and a beautiful hand-sewn white dress. Then her mother went into the bedroom to dress herself. Julie, bored with waiting, went outside to play. It had just rained and there was an inviting puddle in the front lawn. She splashed happily in the oozing mud. When her mother saw Julie's spattered dress, shoes, and socks, she gave a great gasp, then hauled Julie into the house and spanked her.

This was before the era of Dr. Spock, and corporal punishment was the primary form of discipline in the family. Afterward there was no hug and kiss to make up. If her mother hugged her, it was only a part of the nightly ritual, when she would kiss her mother before going to bed.

One of the things that particularly annoyed her mother was when Julie talked too much in front of company—when she "made a display" of herself. Punishment always seemed particularly unjust on these occasions. It wasn't as though she had stolen something, or kicked someone; she was being struck for wanting attention, every child's right and need. The only way she could get approval from her mother was by demanding no attention at all.

When she was about six, a neighboring couple offered

to take her with their children to see Marjoe, the child preacher. This family was Baptist and had invited her to go along, even though she was Catholic, simply because they felt she might enjoy Marjoe. Julie, feeling sure her mother would object to her going to an Evangelist meeting, nevertheless dared to ask permission. At first her mother said no, then gave in.

Julie adored Marjoe. She enjoyed watching as the little boy, about her own age, held a group of adults spellbound with his high-energy enthusiasm. The second she was dropped off at her home, she raced to tell her mother about him. Her mother was sitting in the rocking chair in the kitchen.

"Marjoe was wonderful!" Julie cried. "I loved him. I—"

Her mother looked up from her reading and said, "You're hysterical. Go to bed."

Later Julie realized how depressed her mother must have been all those years, abandoned by her husband, bringing up four children by herself, feeling different from all the other women in town.

She was not a bad mother, not a mean person, but a victim of her life; she could not help what she did. She wanted "the best" for all her children, whatever that meant. She did many things for Julie to make her happy. Julie remembered the little tea parties her mother arranged for her stuffed animals. When Julie went to bed at night she would line up three stuffed animals on each side of her. Each night she changed the order of the animals so no one would feel left out. Her favorite was a fur dog called Wimpy, and she really wanted to go to bed with him alone, but she thought the feelings of the other animals would be hurt, so she slept with them all.

Her mother sewed pretty dresses for her, kept her immaculate, called her "the cleanest child on the block," sometimes changed her dress six times a day. On her birthdays her mother would bake a cake and the family would sing "Happy birthday, dear Julie," and she would burst into tears. She loved the attention but she didn't know how she was supposed to react to it.

She never had close friends as a child; children were naturally scrappy, but she could never slug it out with her playmates because of her mother's restrictions. She felt different, too, because she was taught not to ask for anything, to wait to be invited. When one child had a candy bar, others would say casually, "Give me a bite," but petrified by her instructions to be polite, she never shared the spoils. Once the boy across the street tried to teach her to dance, but he gave up, saying, "It's like trying to drag a log across the floor."

She was scared of everything. Scared of bugs. Scared of birds. Scared of toads. Scared of things that crept or crawled or flew. But she loved her cat, Cabbage.

She hated walking home from school after a rain because of the worms that appeared on the sidewalks. Some of the children, knowing her fear, would pick up a worm and chase her as she ran away screaming. To her, a worm held a terror beyond its nasty appearance, a terror like death.

Julie was saying, on the witness stand, "I have one sister in Michigan, she has a family. I have another sister in California. And I had a brother who killed himself."

Her voice faltered, tears came to her eyes. "I had a brother . . ."

She had seen Allan for the last time in 1962. She had gone home from Chicago for the Fourth of July weekend to visit her mother, but Allan was the one she really wanted to see. He was working as a cook at a resort about ten miles from Port Huron.

She spent a little time talking to her mother, then took the car and drove to Harsens Island. Allan was living in a dormitory with all the others who were working at the resort that summer. There was no private place where Allan and she could talk, so they went to a little bar overlooking the beach. It was called Sans Souci.

Allan ordered beer and smoked. She talked about Chicago for a few minutes, but her chatter was forced. He was obviously disturbed, and she asked him why.

He said he thought he was losing his mind and should be locked up. He was very depressed. He made excuses to avoid seeing friends and spent most of his free time alone. Getting old worried him. He thought his hair was falling out, and he needed glasses but was afraid to have his eyes tested. He felt confused and guilty about not wanting to see or talk to their mother. He mentioned a woman he'd loved but didn't marry. He told Julie about meeting their father, how they would have a drink and play at being pals, and later, after he left his father, he'd want to heave his guts out. He said he felt his whole life had become a façade.

Julie couldn't say anything. Was this really her brother talking? Allan, who was so funny, always made her laugh, had many friends, went to parties, swam, played tennis? Who was this frightened person talking about mental hospitals?

She realized she'd never really known him. When they were children he'd treated her like the pesky little sister she probably was, never wanting her around when his friends came to the house, teasing her, locking her out of his room. Sometimes he'd let her come with him on his paper route and occasionally, when she begged and promised not to cry this time when she lost, he'd play Monopoly with her. But they weren't really friends. It was only after they'd both grown up and left home that they became close. While he was in the Navy submarine service and she was in Chicago, they exchanged letters. Later, when he returned to Port Huron, she'd see him whenever she went home for holidays.

He had a sailboat and a motorboat docked in the St. Clair River. He water-skied, tried to teach her, was not too successful, but they had fun.

It was Allan who taught her to drive. He owned an old '38 Packard he'd won in a poker game. She'd never forget the first time she saw it. He came to visit her one Sunday when she was in boarding school. The girls, watching from the window to see who was having visitors, giggled as they saw the relic make its way up the drive and park beside the Lincolns and Cadillacs. She'd giggled too until she realized the driver of this ridiculous car was her brother. She refused to go anywhere with him in it. He laughed, told her she was a beastly little snob.

Allan shared her pleasure in food and was becoming a good cook. She sent him *Gourmet* and on her visits home he'd always prepare something special. She usually showed her appreciation by eating too much and getting ill. He tried to explain to her the difference between "gourmet" and "gourmand."

Sitting together at the piano, they would compose songs they thought howlingly funny. The melody was usually some variation on "Chopsticks."

Their mother was alarmed by their closeness. She asked Julie to promise never to live with Allan, no matter what happened. "O.K., I promise." Just as she had promised never to take a drink, always to be a good girl, not to make her mother unhappy the way the other children had.

It was easy for Julie to keep this last promise. On July 22, five days before his thirty-second birthday, Allan asphyxiated himself in his car.

She never knew why, and never guessed. It felt wrong to speculate about the motives of the dead, to come up with neat explanations that could be neither confirmed nor contradicted.

He left no note, nothing. When people asked Julie why he committed suicide, she told them, "Because he was unhappy."

At the funeral she shed not one tear. Somehow this would have put her in the camp with the rest of the people Allan had left behind. She held her breath and despised them all.

Cohen was saying, "After you graduated from high school in Port Huron, Michigan, did you move to Chicago?"

"Yes. . . ."

In the fall after she finished high school, her mother decided to go to Florida again to visit her sister. They closed the small house in Port Huron and set out for St. Petersburg.

At first Julie liked Florida, the colorful flowers, the blue waters of the Gulf of Mexico. There had been no jobs in Port Huron for her, but, to her surprise, she got work at once at a brokerage house in St. Petersburg, on Beach Drive. She learned how to chalk the latest stock market prices on a blackboard, though she never understood what the symbols and numbers meant. Usually the room in which she worked was crowded with elderly men and women who watched the blackboard avidly.

In the spring her mother decided to return to Port Huron. Julie stayed in St. Petersburg, even though it was scarcely a city for young people. She had made no friends, but she had no friends in Port Huron, either. She rented a room in a private house. The family seemed pleasant enough, but she would have nothing to do with them. She lost a lot of weight that spring because she skipped suppers, not wanting to eat alone. It was as if she went on a fast the moment her mother left her.

She was not prepared for the intense heat that came with summer. It was more than she could stand, and so were the mammoth mosquitoes, the large furry spiders, and the big beetles Floridians call palmetto bugs. She did not know whether or not they bit, but the sight of them was enough. Sting rays and crabs made it impossible for her to swim in the Gulf; she preferred the rocks of Lake Huron, where no ugly sea creatures bit or stung. In July she rejoined her mother in the town where she never had a date, never had been asked to a high school dance.

The summer started out luckily. Her mother noticed

an ad in the newspaper for help wanted at a new ice cream parlor, and pointed it out to her.

"I'll never get it," Julie said.

"Go down and try," said her mother.

She found a line a block long of boys and girls waiting to be interviewed for the twelve available jobs. To her astonishment, she was chosen as one of the twelve, and she felt jubilant. It was the first time in her life she had been singled out of a large group of people for an honor.

But an ice cream parlor was the last place she should have worked. The owner told the employees, "Eat as much as you want. Free. You'll be sick of ice cream in a week."

Everyone *was* sick of ice cream in a week—except Julie. She ate it all day, and when she left in the evening she took a cone with her. She started out wearing a size twelve uniform, before long had to buy a size fourteen, then a sixteen. She could look down and almost see herself growing. She would tell herself, You've got to stop this, but she could not. She thought of those months as the summer she tried to commit suicide with a spoon.

Cohen was saying, "Could you tell us briefly, please, what you did in Chicago and what your circumstances were there?"

"I lived in Chicago about four years. . . ."

So much had happened in Chicago, both good and bad.

She was going to be an interior decorator. Her father thought it was a great idea and gave her money to go to school there for two years. He said she could not have her own apartment but had to live in the school's dormitory, on Lake Shore Drive between Cedar and Elm. The location was lovely, and she decided it was better than living alone in an apartment.

School was boring. Sometimes she went to classes, most times she didn't. Music students lived on the top floor of the building, and she spent more hours with them than with students from her own school. On Fridays they would all go to hear the Chicago Symphony at Orchestra Hall. It cost only a dollar if you went in the afternoon and sat far up in the balcony, close to the ceiling. She had never had much exposure to classical music, and at first she listened only to melodies. Later she was able to appreciate the styles of different artists. She loved Glenn Gould's Bach, hated what Rosalyn Tureck did to him. This was an exciting time of discovery.

Carrie, one of the music students, gave her lessons on an old piano at the dormitory. She was quick to learn and Carrie urged her to apply to music school. She doubted her father would go for this idea. He had been very disappointed when she told him of her latest learning fiasco. He thought if she wasn't going to school she should find a job. This seemed fair, but what could she do?

She considered herself fortunate when she was hired as a salesgirl at Marshall Field. She enjoyed working there; the woman who ran the department was nice to her, told her she was doing a good job. She loved hearing this, and would have done anything for this woman. Better to hear you're doing a terrific job selling blouses at Marshall Field than to be yelled at for failing algebra two years in a row. She worked there a little over a year.

She was still living at the dormitory, and during this time a friend introduced her to Anton. He was the first man she'd ever dated. His family was in Lebanon and he was studying architecture in Chicago. They saw each other a couple of times a week, usually on weekends.

She now had a boy friend and the status that went with being half of a couple. When the girls sat around the dormitory gossiping or complaining about their love lives, she didn't feel quite so left out, but she still did more listening than talking. When sex came into the conversation she was sure the girls were mostly bluffing. No one really did it until she was married.

The first time for her was with Anton in a hotel on North Clark Street. They'd been going together almost four months. She had clung to her virtue in the belief that nice girls "didn't," and Anton countered with the ancient litany, "If you *really* loved me you would."

The hotel looked like a set for a Tennessee Williams play. The night porter took them up to the room. He refused to give them the key, saying they didn't need it because they probably wouldn't be there long. She wanted to die of shame.

There were three different patterns of worn linoleum on the floor and one naked light bulb hanging on a cord from the ceiling. It was summer, hot. Someone had propped open the window with a beer bootle.

They lay down on the bed. H-O-T-E-L flashed on and off in red neon letters outside the window. It was the year of crinoline petticoats. She was wearing several and didn't want to take them off. Anton teased her, saying her attire looked like a storm on the high seas.

There was very little time. Curfew at the dormitory was eleven. They made love while she bit her wrist. He wanted her to look but she lay facing the wall. She thought, Please, God, is it over now?

This was the first man she'd slept with and in a few months he would be the man she'd marry. For a Catholic girl, these events were definitely out of order. But by the time they were married she had relaxed enough with Anton to enjoy sex with him.

They were married on a cold day in November. Julie, wearing a short Lanz dress (borrowed for the occasion) and a little fur hat (also borrowed), looked quite elegant, but peculiar. The dress and hat were black. At the time it didn't occur to her that this was an odd color for a bride to wear, but after she and Anton were no longer living together she wondered if it had been an omen.

She never told anyone in her family that she was married. Anton's being a "foreigner" would have upset her mother. For her, this was the essence of his charm.

The first few months were happy. They dined on pizza, went to movies, drank espresso, read the same books, made love, made plans. But the plans didn't work out. Anton was irresponsible about money, spending all of his and hers too. Soon their life became a constant struggle.

After about a year they decided to separate. Anton went to New York and she moved to Old Town, Chicago's Greenwich Village. During the eight months they were apart, the telephone bills were enormous. They both remembered the good times, forgot the bad. Anton sent her plane fare and she met him in New York.

It was New Year's Eve, 1963. They joined the crowds in Times Square, holding tight to each other, cheering as they watched the ball descend on the *Times* building, counting the seconds until midnight. Everyone sang "Auld Lang Syne." It seemed an auspicious time for a new beginning.

Anton found a place for them to live on Seventy-ninth Street and York Avenue. It was not really an apartment, just a room. It contained a bed, a cardboard clothes closet, a dresser, and a small table covered with blue speckled contact paper. Plastic flowered curtains hung at the windows, which looked out on an air shaft, so even in the daytime the only light came from a round fluorescent fixture on the wall. But, she thought, it would do while they looked for a better place.

Six months later they were still living there. Anton wasn't home very much, so he didn't care where they lived.

One weekend in July while he was out of the city visiting relatives she left him again, this time for good.

Cohen was asking, "And you were divorced sometime in 1964 or '65?"

"In 1965, I believe," Julie said.

"Was that in New York?"

"Yes. . . ."

Bob knew this because he had been her lawyer for the divorce. A friend had introduced her to one of the senior partners in a prominent New York law firm, who referred her case to an associate, and that was Bob.

She liked him immediately. In her imagination attorneys had always been fussy, distant, reserved people (rather like herself). But Bob was warm, interested, amusing. More important, he was a good lawyer. In a few months she was free from a bond that had become meaningless.

Cohen was asking, "When you came to New York, did you become employed?"

"Yes, I worked for *Esquire* magazine from the time I came to New York until I left nine years later."

"Can you tell me, please, what job you held at *Esquire?*"

"I was a secretary in the advertising department."

"Did there come a time when you felt you were in need of psychiatric assistance?"

"Yes," she said.

"Could you describe to His Honor and to the jury what conditions led you to seek psychiatric help?"

"I was extremely depressed. . . ."

Depressed. That just didn't say it. She felt as if she were dying, dead, withered inside. She wished she could evaporate, disappear. She couldn't stand looking at her reflection, so she spray-painted all the mirrors in her apartment. She was appalled if she accidentally caught sight of herself in a glass. This ugly, pale apparition, no makeup, straight brown hair . . . she was grotesque. She hated going to work, hated being at work. She'd sit at her desk and start crying for no apparent reason. She could hardly wait until noon to leave, so she could go home to sleep. Sometimes she'd wake up and go back to the office, sometimes not. Her boss, Evan Forgelman, would always call to see if she was all right. What could she tell him? Even if she told him the truth, "No, I'm not O.K., I'm dying inside," he'd probably say, "You'll feel better tomorrow."

Her friend Anne was the only one who knew how bad it was, the only person she still talked to. Anne said she should go to a therapist, and wanted to make an appointment for her with Dr. Pauline Anderson, a psychologist Anne was seeing. Julie refused but Anne continued to bring up the subject. Coming from anyone else it would have been nagging, but she knew Anne loved her. They had been friends nearly ten years.

One reason Anne worried about her was that she had worn the same dress, day after day, for the past two years. It was a Marimekko, one of those printed cotton dresses from Finland, full and flowing. Hers was knee-length, with purple flowers patterned on a dark-blue background. Its style was plain except for three silver buttons on the left shoulder. It had cost her $56.

Julie felt very much attached to the dress and had already patched it in four places. Though old and worn, it was always clean. Recently, thinking she really should have a change of clothing, she had bought two new Marimekkos. The tags still hung on them; she did not feel like herself in the new dresses. The dark blue was familiar, she knew how she looked in it to herself and other people, and it hid what she thought of as her ugly shape.

Julie had met Anne in 1961 when they both lived on Chicago's Gold Coast, near the Ambassador Hotel, in the elegant graystone mansion that had been the Astor home. Anne lived in the turret, and from it she and Julie would watch furred and bejeweled ladies going to parties in the Hugh Hefner home across the way. They often went out to dinner, movies, concerts, listened to music late at night as they talked of their dreams. They shared ice cream and bread binges—Julie liked the

crusty outsides and Anne the doughy insides. Anne was
then studying acting at the Goodman Theatre School,
but after she came to New York she turned to art. She
took classes in printmaking, illustration, and sculpture
at night school and worked during the day at a variety
of jobs, clerking at Brentano's, hostessing at Mama
Leone's. She went to Italy for the year of 1965, married in 1967, and was now separating from her husband.

Anne had had a difficult time trusting a therapist, but
thought the prospect of getting help was worth a try.
Now Julie thought, well, why *not* see Anne's therapist?
Psychotherapy will be my last stop before killing myself. She knew she would make no suicide "attempt,"
but would succeed once she made the decision to destroy herself. She thought about suicide a good deal of
the time; the thought made her daily life bearable. That
her brother had taken his life removed some of the
stigma from it. She would tell herself, You have a way
of ending this misery if you choose. But now she said to
herself, Hang in there a little longer, see if professional
help can't get you out of this depression.

Even music was no longer a pleasure. She had always
wanted a piano, and when earlier she received $2,500
from the new owner of her apartment house, who
wanted her to move out, she had bought the first luxury
of her life, an upright Steinway, and started to take
lessons. She still took lessons but her enjoyment in them
was gone.

She constantly felt like crying. She would be walking
along the street, or riding a bus, or sitting at her desk,
and inexplicably burst into tears. She would cry as if
her heart were breaking, though there was no one in her
life to break it.

The only man to whom she was friendly was Evan, her understanding boss. When she had first arrived in the city she went directly to *Esquire* with a letter written by a friend in Chicago who knew an *Esquire* executive. She was hired on the spot because Evan, who needed a secretary, thought her bright and attractive, and liked her efficient manner.

"I don't know shorthand," she said apologetically.

"I'll use a dictaphone," he offered.

"But I don't know how to use a dictaphone," she said.

"We'll work out something," he reassured her.

He got a dictaphone but found he disliked it and she had trouble using it, so he wrote everything in longhand and she learned to read his writing. He was not always the easiest person in the world to get along with, as he would be the first to admit, but they respected each other. He excused her eccentricities, knowing she would somehow finish her work. He gave her steady raises and advanced her from secretary to promotion assistant, though she had little interest in climbing the ladder in the advertising department, doing work she considered inconsequential. The very goal of advertising went against her nature—trying to persuade consumers they could not live without expensive products they did not need. Her work gave her no satisfaction.

She felt she had nothing in New York. She had nothing, period. What reason was there for living when you were paralyzed in feeling and act? She did not feel stifled, for that meant you had ideas to express that were bottled up. She felt *empty,* not even aware of how she would like her life to change. She thought of herself as a melancholy person, doomed to sadness. Anne, on the other hand, thought it possible to change; that was why she had gone into therapy. Julie finally told Anne to go ahead, try to make an appointment for her to see Anne's therapist.

One evening she was sleeping, dreamless, when the phone rang. She picked it up and heard Anne's voice.

"You have an appointment with Dr. Anderson on Thursday at five, Julie."

"O.K."

She felt too drained to be excited, too tired even to thank Anne for what she had done.

"Will you be all right, Julie?" Anne asked.

"I'll live until Thursday."

"Good girl. I'll call you later." Anne hung up.

She placed the receiver in its cradle and sank back on the pillow. She thought she might wear one of the new Marimekko dresses when she saw Dr. Anderson. A lot was riding on this, her first visit to a therapist.

2

Cohen was saying, "Now, Julie, what did you do about getting help for your problems?"

"I went to Dr. Anderson. . . ."

Dr. Pauline Anderson was a psychologist who saw patients in her apartment on East Thirteenth Street, off Second Avenue. She was slight of build, with gray hair, and she greeted Julie warmly, then led her into a small room that held, in addition to books, an Afghan dog and a Siamese cat.

Julie sat in a chair facing Dr. Anderson, who lit a cigarette. Julie did not smoke.

Dr. Anderson encouraged her to talk, and she told Dr. Anderson of her depression, how most of the time she slept, cried, or thought of killing herself.

"I am so unhappy," she said. "I thought maybe you could help me."

"I can't treat you," Dr. Anderson said, "because your closest friend is my patient. But I will refer you to someone."

Julie felt an unaccustomed surge of anger. Why hadn't Dr. Anderson told her this before she opened herself up, revealed what a pathetic creature she was? She felt she had been deceived.

"Forget it!"

She stood up and walked out of the office.

The dreary days of fall passed, and then the sadness that was Christmas. She was still forcing herself to go to work every day, but she kept suicide in a corner of her mind. The inertia that possessed her seemed to hold her back from taking her own life.

Anne tried for months to persuade her to call Dr. Anderson and get the name of another therapist, but Julie emphatically refused.

One cold night there came another telephone call from Anne.

"I have the name of the psychiatrist Dr. Anderson wants you to see," Anne said. "You must call him, Julie. You can't go on like this."

"I don't want to see anyone," she said.

"Please, Julie. You have to."

"I can't."

Anne kept after her, in a quietly insistent way. One night when Anne was visiting her, again pleading, Julie gave in. "O.K. What's his name?"

Anne pulled a slip of paper out of her purse and read from it. "Dr. Renatus Hartogs."

Anne handed her the paper, saying, "Here's his address and telephone number. You'll have to call for an appointment."

Julie stared at the paper.

"Shall I call for you?" Anne asked.

"No," said Julie. "I'll do it."

The next afternoon when she got home from work, she took off her tan trench coat, went to the telephone, and dialed the number on the slip of paper.

She was surprised to hear a man's voice say, "Hello." She had expected a nurse or answering service.

"My name is Julie Roy," she said. "I'd like to make

an appointment to see Dr. Hartogs." She hoped her voice did not reveal her inner trembling.

"Who referred you?" the man asked.

"Dr. Pauline Anderson," she said.

"Just a minute and I'll look at my appointment book," said the man. He had a thick accent, which she thought intriguing, in keeping with her mental picture of psychiatrists.

There was a pause, then, "Could you come next Saturday at three P.M.?"

"Yes," she said.

She would have assented had he said three A.M.

Cohen was asking, "Do you remember your first visit to Dr. Hartogs' office?"

"Yes," she said. "It was not a very long visit and I remember crying."

For her first appointment with a psychiatrist she dressed carefully, slipping on the dark-blue Marimekko, then her trench coat. She always kept the coat on when she was with other people, even indoors, because she was self-conscious about her weight. She dreaded the coming of summer, when she would have to take off the coat.

She took the Madison Avenue bus uptown from her apartment to Seventy-ninth Street. Dr. Hartogs' office was east of Madison on Seventy-eighth. The entrance, a few steps from the corner, was of white stucco with a white pillar on each side of the wide glass door. Above the door, carved in the stucco was the information "No. 39." A white plate on the right side of the door bore the name "Dr. Renatus Hartogs" in black. She thought, I like the name, it sounds appropriate for a psychiatrist.

She went through the outer door and rang the buzzer next to Dr. Hartogs' name on the wall. An answering buzz opened the locked inner door. In the foyer she saw an elevator and a flight of stairs. She chose the stairs.

She walked up slowly, feeling a slight sense of panic at the thought of seeing this psychiatrist. She did not know what she was getting into, did not want to talk about her feelings to a strange man even though he was supposed to be a mental healer with a medical degree. Perhaps he could just give her a pill to make her feel better.

On the second floor, she found a door with his name on it. As she opened it she noticed on the doorjamb a mezuzah, a Jewish talisman with prayers inside. She walked in.

A narrow hallway faced her. To her left she saw, to her surprise, a small kitchen. Farther along to her left she came upon a room filled with at least a dozen people —men, women, and one little boy. They were all sitting except the boy and his father, who were standing because there were not enough chairs.

Have I made a mistake? she thought. What are all these people doing here? I thought a psychiatrist was supposed to see each patient for fifty minutes. Perhaps I've stumbled into a dentist's office by mistake.

She stood, along with the boy and the man. In about five minutes the door to an inner office was opened by a man dressed in black slacks, shirt and tie, no jacket. He was short, slightly plumper than average, with a barrel-like chest.

"Who's next?" the man said, speaking with the accent she recalled from the telephone conversation.

Her first impression was that he seemed very self-confident. His eyes were blue, intense, and piercing. His hair, a fringe around his head, was gray, as were his muttonchop sideburns and his bushy eyebrows. She thought his mouth rather thin.

There was no receptionist. The patients kept track of who came next. Soon a chair was empty and she sat down. She was too anxious to read any of the magazines that lay on a table nearby. As the patients went in and out, she noticed Dr. Hartogs did not greet anyone by name. Some patients stayed inside only a few minutes, some as long as twenty. When they left, she saw them bypass the waiting room as they walked down the corridor on their way out.

She thought again, I *cannot* be in a psychiatrist's office, this *must* be a dentist's office. When I telephoned for an appointment, the voice asked only, "Who referred you?" so I might have been calling about a toothache.

Finally after what seemed two hours, it was her turn. When Dr. Hartogs asked, "Who's next?" she stood up and followed him. She walked through a small foyer between the waiting room and his office and saw, to its left, a bathroom.

As she stepped into his office she blinked. The walls looked dark; black linen drapes were pulled across the two windows so no light filtered in. There was only one light in the room, a lamp on his desk with a solid shade reflecting the light downward. She did not object to the darkness; she felt at home in places that were cavelike, like her own apartment.

Dr. Hartogs' desk was on the right side of the room, with one chair behind it, a second in front. Along a wall bookcases rose high, atop them African sculptures. She particularly admired the head of a man carved in dark wood. There were a typewriter and chair in one corner. Across the room, to her left, sat a couch covered in black cotton fabric with a matching pillow. A chair was placed at the right of the couch, and between couch and chair there was a sun lamp. The doors of two closets stood at the sides of the desk, like sentinels.

An impressive array of diplomas and certificates of membership in various organizations framed in black hung on the walls. To the left of the desk she saw a small picture of Freud.

Before she sat down she asked, "What kind of doctor are you?"

"What kind of doctor are you looking for?" he said.

If she said "psychiatrist" and he turned out to be a dentist, she would be very embarrassed. Afraid she had made a mistake, and not wanting to appear foolish, she said, "A dentist."

"I'm a psychiatrist," he said, a touch of humor in his voice. "Did you want to see me?"

"Yes." She could hardly get the word out, but thought, He must know how frightened I am, he will understand.

He directed her to sit in the chair facing him across the desk. She had to turn the chair slightly to the right in order to get into it, and she left the chair angled that way so she would not have to look directly into those intense eyes.

She noticed the chair in which he sat because it was so unusual. It was like a throne, or a chair at the head of a manor-house dining table. Its high back, of elaborately carved wood framing a golden velvet fabric, rose at least a foot above his head. She would have preferred a more equal seating arrangement; she felt inferior perched in a small Danish modern chair in her trench coat.

"Don't you want to take off your coat?" he asked.

"No, thank you." She did not want him to see her fat body.

He took out a blank white card, asked, "What's your name?"

"Julie Ellen Roy."

He wrote it down. "What's your address?"

She gave him her address and telephone number.

"Age?"

"Thirty."

"Married?"

"Divorced."

"Where were you born?"

"Port Huron, Michigan."

"Why do you want to see a psychiatrist?" he asked, putting away the white card.

"Because I'm so depressed and unhappy," she said. "I feel like crying all the time." She was reluctant to talk about herself. "Perhaps some sort of medication would help me."

He took a pad, wrote out two prescriptions, handed them to her. One was for Dexamyl spansules, the other for Triavil tablets.

"Where do you work?" he asked.

She told him that she had started as a secretary at *Esquire* but was now a promotion assistant in the advertising department.

"How much do you make?" he asked.

"One hundred and seventy-five dollars a week."

"What do you think you can pay for treatment?"

She hesitated, then said, "Twenty-five dollars a week." Considering her other expenses, including rent of $200 a month and her weekly music lessons, that seemed all she could afford.

"I usually charge more but I'll see you three times a week at ten dollars a session," he said.

"O.K." She would manage the extra $5. "Thank you."

He consulted his appointment book. "I can see you next Wednesday at four. That will be ten dollars for this session."

She was surprised at this sudden dismissal, but thought, I have bored him, depression is boring, and after fifteen minutes he can't stand me any longer.

She wrote out a check for $10, gave it to him. Then she stood up and walked out of his office through the door that led to the outer corridor. Slowly she descended the flight of steps to the first floor, feeling she had made a nuisance of herself.

She started to cry as she was going down the stairs. There was an open place behind the stairs where she could hide and, she hoped, not be noticed. She crept under the stairs and cried quietly, as she sometimes had done as a girl when she did not want her mother to hear. She hoped no one would see her and think she was crazy.

For some reason, as she cried, she thought of her father, and the July day when he had left the house. She remembered her mother crying as she rearranged the dining-room chairs, telling Allan, then twelve years old, "You sit at the head of the table. You're head of the family now."

Once her father left, he never came back to see them. He acted as if he didn't care what happened to them, though he did give them money. Her mother alternated between a burning hatred for him and outbursts of crying over being deserted.

Her father later married another woman, had one child, then left them too. Julie recalled him as an aloof man wno never picked her up, never showed affection. She was sure he had never wanted her—she came along eight years after Allan, and by then her father obviously was not getting along with her mother. He never put up a battle for custody of the children, as other fathers did. She could only conclude he did not want any of his children. Once in a while, as she was growing up, she would run into her father on the street in Port Huron, and they would say hello like remote acquaintances.

She had a clear memory of her mother telling her as a child to stay out of the living room if her father was there, reading or listening to the radio. She could hear her mother saying, "Keep out of your father's way, Julie, don't be a nuisance." When her father left, it never occurred to her to mourn; she only thought that now she could go into the living room whenever she wanted.

Her mother always instructed her, when she went to the home of a friend, to be sure to leave when the father came home, because a family didn't want outsiders around. Even now, when she visited a friend who was married, she felt she had to leave when the husband came home. When one of her girl friends would occasionally see her father, Julie would feel consumed by a great jealousy, especially when the father brought his daughter a gift. And whenever women mentioned their attachment to their fathers, she felt unhappy and withdrawn.

While growing up she told herself that the person who fathered her was not important, because he was out of her life for so many years. She thought "father" a word that meant nothing to her. When her sister Carol informed her that their father had died, she heard this with the same emotion as if Carol had told her California was suffering a dry spell; the fact seemed unrelated to her. But she wondered at times if her father's absence from home did not leave black holes in her personality, even though she was not conscious of them.

She remembered the one time her father had kissed her—on the lips. She felt appalled rather than pleased, as though a stranger were kissing her. She had been in the hospital in Port Huron recovering from a tonsillectomy at the age of twelve, and did not expect her father to visit.

When she was fifteen and sixteen, once in a while, perhaps half a dozen times in all, her father came to the house to take her out to dinner. She would sit quietly through the meal, speaking when spoken to, being polite, never asking the questions she wanted to ask, like why he had left his family.

She saw her father as a man governed by his whims, lacking nobility or strength. One of her aunts once spoke of him in contempt as "a race-track tout" because he occasionally bet on horses. Her mother was not so concerned with the money he lost as with his not living up to her image of the "respectable" family man. He didn't take the family out on Sundays or fix things around the house.

She did not recall any hysterical arguments between her mother and father, only one mild fight as they were parting. It was over a metal box. Her mother insisted the box belonged to her, her father insisted it was his. And, she thought, gallant man that he was, my father took the box. Just once she heard her mother faintly praise him; she did not remember clearly what for. She thought her mother had called him "cocky" because he was not afraid to drive in the days of prohibition, when cars in northern Michigan were being hijacked to drive to Canada and transport liquor illegally back across the border.

But she had not been without masculine affection when she was a child. She remembered a black mailman named Archie who would walk up the front path to put letters into the mailbox attached to the front door. One day she was sitting on the steps as Archie passed, and he patted her on the head. Thereafter, every day the mail was delivered, she sat on those steps, rain or shine, so Archie would pat her on the head. She noticed that if there were no mail, Archie would merely wave as he passed in front of the house. So then she went out and sat on the part of the lawn that edged the sidewalk, waiting for him each day. She thought maybe her early affection for Archie was the reason that, when she felt very lonely, she went to a jazz place frequented by black men.

She had been alone with her mother ever since she was nine. The other children, before they left home, were more of an age. She felt she had no one. She never could mix with strange children because she felt like a freak, she had no father. On school forms where she had to fill in the blank that said, "Father's name," she always wrote, "No father." "What's this, Julie? No father's name?" She would say, "I never had a father."

The other children would tease her, chanting, "Julie has no daddy," telling her she had no right to the name Roy, she should use her mother's maiden name, and she would run home crying, as she was now doing.

When she faced Dr. Hartogs on Wednesday, having once again waited her turn, she handed him the bottles containing the two prescription drugs.

"They didn't do me any good," she said, surprised to hear a somewhat defiant note in her voice. "Give them to some other patient."

He accepted the drugs.

She had decided to try to talk to him about her feelings. It would be difficult; she had always felt she was not really entitled to have any feelings, much less speak of them. But for the first time in her life, she believed she had found someone willing to listen to her.

He did not ask questions but waited for her to speak. So, haltingly she began. "I have this problem of over-eating."

She was unable to lose weight, could not draw up those obsessive little diet lists and stick to them. The quickest way for her to put on weight was to worry about it. She worried a lot—and ate mountains of ice cream and tons of bread, her two nemeses.

"I hate myself because I can't eat sensibly," she said.

He offered no advice. At the end of what seemed like ten minutes, he said, "I can see you next Friday at five."

She wrote a check for $10 thinking, He is only seeing me two times this week. Why did he suggest three?

Cohen was asking, "Julie, what occurred starting in March, 1969, when you began to visit Dr. Hartogs in his office on a regular basis in connection with this psychiatric consultation?"

She said, "I cried a lot and I tried to talk to Dr. Hartogs about what was bothering me. Dr. Hartogs' first suggestion . . ."

After she entered his office, following the customary wait, he said in what she thought a teasing voice, "Why don't we have a bathtub party?"

She did not know what that meant, but it sounded as though he were proposing sex. She thought, He must be joking, he knows how inhibited I am and this risqué remark is his way of getting me to be more open, for my own good. But she imagined the two of them, naked, sitting in his bathtub, eating—what's a party without food? Apples would be good, they'd float. Cake would be too messy. Then she thought of his biting into an apple with those perfect teeth, worried they might be false, and the idea of a "bathtub party" became repulsive to her. As did the thought of sex—she was thirty and he must be about sixty. She did not find him at all sexy.

She said nothing, pretending not to have heard.

"Tell me your fantasies about me," he said.

"I don't have any," she said.

"You must have some."

"I don't." She did not know how to isolate a fantasy in words.

As she left his office after the regular payment of $10, she thought again about his allusion to a "bathtub party." She could not come right out and tell him she thought the idea was absurd, but she hoped he would make no more such ridiculous suggestions.

Cohen was asking, "Thereafter, did he make any statements to you or do any acts which indicated that he wished to have sex with you?"

"Yes. . . ."

A visit or so later he asked, "How do you feel about me?"

"I don't feel anything," she said.

He looked as though he did not believe her. He put out his hand, said, "Give me your hand."

"Why?" she asked.

"Let's shake hands," he said.

She was wary of touching him but did not want him to think her unfriendly—he might get angry and stop seeing her. She reached out her hand, then drew it back before their hands met. She just could not touch him.

After the ten-minute session ended and, as usual, she handed him the $10 check, she found herself once again crying in the open place under the stairs. For the first time someone saw her, a middle-aged woman waiting for the elevator.

The woman looked startled, then walked over to her and asked, "Is anything wrong? Can I help?"

"No, thank you," she said.

"Would you like to come up for a cup of tea?" asked the woman, evidently a tenant of the building.

"No, thank you. I'll be O.K.," she said.

The woman's kindness got her out from under the stairs a little sooner than otherwise.

A few sessions later Dr. Hartogs said to her, "Let's have sex."

She could not believe her ears. Her psychiatrist propositioning her! Perhaps he was testing her, to see how she would react. Once again she pretended not to hear.

"It will cure you of being a lesbian," he said. "Your trouble is that you are afraid of men."

She had told him of an experience that had caused her great guilt. One day, shortly after she had left her husband, she went to Lord & Taylor to buy a pair of shoes. A salesgirl came up to her and asked, "Can I help you?"

She pointed to a pair of shoes and asked for size 7½, not really noticing the salesgirl. But when the salesgirl came back with the shoes and helped her put them on, they recognized each other. In Chicago they'd both lived in the old Astor mansion. Julie had been married and living with Anton, and the other girl, Chris, had lived alone down the hall. They hadn't really known each other, just said hello as they passed on the stairs. She vaguely remembered that Chris was a "lesbian." Dark, mysterious word. Julie wasn't sure what it meant.

Seeing Chris now, she welcomed the familiar face. They swiftly exchanged stories about how long they'd been in New York, where they lived (Julie was then sharing an apartment with Anne, Chris lived alone in the Village), took each other's phone number. Chris said she'd call. Julie didn't think Chris would.

She saw only the people she worked with, and none of them socially. No one ever called her on the phone, so she was reluctant to answer it when it rang the next evening. What if it was an obscene phone call? But maybe it was for Anne, so she'd have to pick it up.

"Well! Hi! Hello! . . . Yes, I'm surprised. . . . No, I haven't eaten dinner yet. . . . Sure, I'd like to meet you. Italian would be great. . . . You'll pick me up? O.K. It's the renovated place on the corner of Tenth and Avenue B. What kind of car should I look for? A motorcycle! Oh, no. I'm not riding on any motorcycle. . . . Yes, I'm scared. . . . No, absolutely not. I'll meet you there . . . OK., about forty-five minutes. See you."

They met at a little Italian restaurant on Waverly Place. She hardly remembered what they ate, they had so much to say to each other. Chris was vivacious, they laughed, drank a little wine, reminisced about Chicago. Chris knew she had been married, was surprised to learn she had left her husband three months ago and was now living with Anne. She told Chris how she disliked living in New York, that she felt frightened and alone most of the time. Chris was alone, too, though she did not seem unhappy about it, or frightened. She had tremendous confidence and Julie was soon infected with her good spirits.

As they were leaving the restaurant, Chris asked if she'd just look at the motorcycle. She looked, and was surprised to find it small and blue, not big, black, and greasy, as she'd imagined.

"O.K., just around the block, but slowly!"

And it really was fun. It was summer and the night air rushing past her face felt refreshingly cool. They drove around the block, then downtown, under the West Side Highway, and all around the warehouse district where there was no traffic. She kept her arms around Chris's waist, held on tight. Sometimes, to avoid the wind, she'd bury her face in Chris's neck. Chris's blond hair was soft, fragrant. Julie forgot about the wind.

When Chris dropped her in front of her house, she knew Chris would call again. They began spending time together, meeting for lunch and dinner, going mostly to Village places like the Ninth Circle.

Shortly after she began seeing Chris, she came home from work one evening and thought the apartment looked strange. The refrigerator door stood open and her suitcase lay on the living-room floor. The window leading to the fire escape was open.

She stared. Puzzlement. Then shock. "Somebody's been here! We've been robbed!" But who would rob them and why? They had no furniture. She and Anne had been sleeping on the floor, their clothes still in suitcases. They had one valuable item between them—her sewing machine. Actually Singer still owned it, she had made only one payment. Not much in the way of loot, but it was gone.

Suddenly she was scared. It was horrible to know some stranger had been touching your things, pawing through your clothes. She ran out of the apartment, called Chris from a booth on the corner. As soon as Chris arrived, they phoned the police. The police came, looked around, said, "It must have been junkies," and left.

She didn't want to stay in the apartment after that, so she went to Chris's apartment. It was the first time she had been there. Chris's apartment looked clean and cozy, like a home, not like the barren rooms she had just fled.

Chris made dinner while she played with the cat.

They listened to Dylan and ate cheeseburgers by candle-light, drank a little wine, which made her drowsy. She curled up on the couch while Chris cleared the dishes and fussed in the kitchen. It had started to rain. Chris changed the record, some Irish tenor was singing lovely ballads. She felt no desire to move when Chris walked over and sat beside her, touched her hair. They talked, decided she would stay the night.

Chris turned down the covers. The music was soft, the candle still burned, the rain pattered on the windows. Julie lay there, feeling sleepy and content. Chris covered them with a beautiful old quilt. They snuggled, their arms around each other. Chris was kissing her. . . .

She described her involvement with Chris to Dr. Hartogs. He made no comment except to ask her to tell him the details of their sex life. She refused. She wanted to please him, but she was too shy to speak of anything sexual.

A session or two later, he asked, "Why won't you have sex with me?"

"I don't believe you mean it," she said, certain he was mocking her.

"I do," he said.

She felt frightened. "I can't do it."

"Why not?"

"I feel I would be destroyed. That in the end, it would be bad for me." She was being as honest as she knew how.

"It would be good for you," he said. "If you can love me, you can love another man."

She could not escape the intensity of his blue eyes, staring into her own green eyes.

He went on, "It happens because of a process called 'transference.' If you love me, you can then transfer the feeling to other men who are more suitable."

"What do you mean—more suitable?" She was alarmed. Why was he offering himself if he did not feel "suitable"?

Cohen was asking, "Julie, you testified that Dr. Hartogs made a suggestion that you and he have sex together. When, for the first time, did he make such a suggestion?"

"I don't remember the month," she said. "It was within a few weeks after I had started to see him."

"Did he ask you about your problems, ask you to talk about them?"

"He asked me what my problems were. He didn't insist that I talk about them. Most of the things Dr. Hartogs said had something to do with my having a sexual relationship with him."

Samuel Halpern, the defense attorney, rose and said, "Objection to that."

"I will allow it," said Judge Myers. "That phrase, 'something to do with a sexual relationship' is stricken." Turning to Julie, he said, "You will have to be more specific, madam. As best as you can, always give us a particular time sequence and try to recollect the actual words that passed between you and Dr. Hartogs."

Cohen asked if she remembered other statements or acts that indicated Dr. Hartogs wanted to have sex with her.

"Yes," she said. "Dr. Hartogs said I must be much more open about sexual matters. I must be able to discuss these with him. If I would be closer to him physically, it would be easier for me to talk about these things with him, he said. I remember ..."

It was a warm day in April, and her spirits were high for a change. She asked him, "Why am I so horrified by some words?"

She remembered when she was six, her mother had washed her mouth out with soap for using the word "snot." She still gagged when she smelled a bar of Fels Naphtha.

Another time her mother had spanked her with the yardstick when she had scrawled the words "shit," "hell," and "damn" (spelling it "dam") on little white envelopes her mother used for church donations. The whipping hurt for hours. Her mother had forbidden her to say the words but had never told her she could not write them.

She told Dr. Hartogs, "One day when I was living in Chicago, I was walking through the long cement tunnel that leads to the beach under Oak Street. I saw the word 'F-U-C-K,' " she spelled it out, "written in letters three feet high on the wall. I was so upset I turned around and went home. Whenever I walked through the tunnel after that, I'd turn my head so I wouldn't even see the word from the corner of my eye. I could not even look at the word, let alone say it."

Suddenly he said, "Fuck." Loudly.

She gave him a look of horror. Then she stood up, threw down on his desk the check for $10 that she had made out in advance, and said, "I don't want to see you anymore."

She ran out of his office and down the stairs. On the first floor, in her sheltered place, she burst into tears, furious, thinking, How dare he do this to me?

But as she walked away from his building, she felt ashamed of her angry flight. Maybe he had deliberately tried to shock her, to loosen her up. After all, he did not use the word in the context of a conversation or to express emotion. She had acted ridiculously if indeed he had uttered the word for her own good.

Because she had left so abruptly he had not set the next appointment. Suppose he never wanted to see her again? She had been going to him twice a week for five months, she looked forward to every session, she needed him. She had been idiotic to be such a prude.

That night she wrote him, saying she understood he had said the word to help her overcome her inhibitions, she was sorry she had behaved in such a hasty manner, and she would call him to find out the time of her next appointment.

Cohen was asking, "Did Dr. Hartogs tell you why he thought it was important for you to be able to touch him or have a physical relationship with him?"

"Yes, because I would be having a relationship with a man and if we were going to work on my homosexuality it was important that I should have a relationship with a man, he said."

"Did there come a point in time in 1969 when, in fact, you did begin touching Dr. Hartogs, or he began touching you, and you did begin having some sort of physical relationship?"

"Yes," she said.

"And when, approximately, did that occur?"

"April of 1969."

She felt it was a turning point in their relationship when she agreed to take off her trench coat. Now she felt she knew him well enough to let him see the outlines of her body.

But her dress was almost as concealing as the trench coat. By this time the Marimekko had patch number five, but she loved it as much as ever.

To take up the usual ten minutes, she rambled on once again about her ever present weight problem. As she prepared to leave, she picked up the trench coat. To her surprise, he swiftly stood up from his desk, came behind her, and helped her on with it. As he slipped it over her shoulders, he gave her a gentle hug.

She was embarrassed, did not know what to say or do, so she laughed as though the act were humorous. She was frightened, though, for this was his first real touch, the start of a commitment.

It became a routine, sort of a dance, each time she prepared to leave. He would get up from his desk, walk around to give her a goodbye hug. She would try to anticipate the moment when he would rise so she could race him to the door and escape the embrace.

One day she rose from the wrong side of her chair and found him standing between her and the door. She took two steps backward, he took two steps forward. She took another two steps backward, he took another two steps forward.

Two more steps and she found herself halfway inside one of the closets behind his desk. There was no place for her to move.

He came close, put his arms around her, leaned forward, kissed her on the lips. At first she resisted, then she started to respond to his warmth.

As he let her go, he said, "I knew you would be like this." She thought there was a note of triumph in his voice.

"How did you know?" she asked.

"I knew it from the first time you walked into the office," he said. Then he added, "I love you, darling."

It was a day to remember, she thought, the day her psychiatrist told her he loved her.

From then on, each session, he would either stand up and kiss her goodbye or remain in his chair and say, "Give me a kiss goodbye."

She felt all the kissing and hugging could lead only to trouble. He could not possibly be in love with her; she was only one of his many woman patients. Yet his pursuit of her made her feel quite desirable. What woman would not want to be thought attractive, especially by her psychiatrist?

Cohen was asking, "During these early sessions, in March and April, approximately how long did each session take?"

"Somewhere between five and twenty minutes," she said.

He asked, "Now, Julie, do you recall any incidents where Dr. Hartogs touched any part of your body?"

"Yes," she said. "One time . . ."

He stood up and walked over to where she sat. To her amazement, he knelt down in front of her. Then he put his hands on her legs, caressed them.

"I love your legs," he said. "I notice them when you come in and when you leave."

She felt very embarrassed, but did not know what to say. It wasn't as if some strange lecher came up to her on a bus and touched her legs. This man was her *doctor,* he had been giving her therapy for six months, he was the man she was supposed to trust above all others.

She sat stiffly in her chair, looked at him with fear.

He stood up, indicating her ten-minute hour was at an end.

Cohen was asking, "Did there come a point of time when he and you had conversations concerning your lying on the couch?"

She said, "The first time that happened . . ."

It was May, the trees were starting to green, and New York seemed almost a beautiful place, she thought as she entered his office.

"Where would you be more comfortable," he asked, "on the couch or in the chair?"

Startled, she said, "In the chair."

"Wouldn't you rather lie down on the couch?" he asked. "I'll lie down with you."

"Both of us?" She was shocked.

"It's more comfortable," he said. "You'll see."

He led her to the black couch. She sat down on it.

"Stretch out," he said.

Fearfully, she lay back. He placed himself beside her. She felt excited at the thought her doctor wanted to be that close to her.

"There, isn't that better?" he said, his shoulder touching hers, his hips touching hers.

She tried not to feel anything. "Why are we doing this?" she asked.

He explained once again that it was important for her to establish physical contact with a man because her sexual orientation was toward women. If she was going to be "cured," she had to get accustomed to a man's body. He added, "If we are close physically, it will make it easier for you to talk."

She could not think of a single word to say.

Cohen was asking, "Did there come a time when either you or Dr. Hartogs began disrobing before you would lie on the couch in his office?"

"Dr Hartogs was the first one to take his clothing off," she said.

Judge Myers asked, "When did that happen?"

"In May of 1969," she said.

Cohen asked, "In those sessions in May, after Dr. Hartogs took his clothes off, did you begin to take your clothes off?"

"Yes. . . ."

They lay on the couch together, as they had been doing each session, and he asked her to have sex with him, as he had been doing each session, and, as she had been doing each session, she refused.

Then he said, "Don't you want to take your clothes off?"

"Why?" She felt even more shocked than at his use of the word "fuck." He said, "Some psychiatrists will only treat their patients when they are nude. You shouldn't be so ashamed of your body. You should be less inhibited about it. You'll be much more comfortable with your clothes off."

"I wouldn't be comfortable without my clothes," she said, thinking, What is he up to? Does he believe all this nonsense is going to help me?

Then he asked, "Do you want to see the kind of underwear I wear?"

"Why would I?" she said.

"Because it's very unusual for a man's underwear."

"No." She was afraid he would display more than his underwear.

"I'm going to show you," he said, standing up.

"No, I don't want you to expose yourself," she said.

"I promise I won't," he said.

He unbuckled his belt. She turned her eyes away.

"Look!" he commanded.

Slowly, reluctantly, she turned her head.

He stood there in black shorts.

"It's black bikini underwear," he said.

She had seen the advertisement in *Esquire,* so they were not entirely new to her.

She rose from the couch as though to say, That's enough, and he put on his trousers.

Cohen was asking, "Did there come a time that you began to disrobe and lie on the couch with him?"

"Yes...."

Before he lay down on the couch he took off his trousers. He explained, "I don't want them to wrinkle," and draped them over the chair next to the couch.

Then he said, "Don't you want to take off your dress?"

"No! No!" she said.

She felt foolish that she had allowed him to persuade her to go this far, and was afraid of what might happen if she removed her dress.

Then he was taking off his shirt as well as his trousers, so he wore only the black bikinis; his barrel-like chest showed bare and hairy. He had a tan skin tone, and she thought he must spend time under the sun lamp to give himself added bronze color.

He said, "I don't feel very comfortable with you lying there dressed. Why don't you take off your clothes?"

She held out for a few sessions but at one point when he disrobed and asked once again, "Why don't you take off your dress?" she must have looked at him with an air of surrender, for he started to lift the dress up over her head.

Oh, she thought, what's the difference? She finished taking off the Marimekko, tossing it on the chair next to his trousers and shirt. Then she lay down beside him in her panties and bra.

He turned to her, kissed her on the lips, fondled her breasts. She pushed his hands away. Then he placed her hand on his penis. She withdrew it as soon as he lifted his hand.

She said, "I don't think this is such a good idea."

"Don't you like me?" he asked.

"Yes," she said, not really sure how she felt about him.

"Aren't you glad you're with me instead of with a woman?"

"Yes," she said, afraid to say no.

Cohen was asking, "Did you and Dr. Hartogs continue to lie on the couch, both of you with your underwear on?"

"Yes," she said.

"Did there come a point where either you or Dr. Hartogs had your underwear taken off?"

"Yes."

"Approximately when did that occur?"

"June of 1969."

"Through May and June of 1969, did you continue paying Dr. Hartogs for each visit that you had?"

"Yes."

"How were you generally feeling during this period of time?"

"I was not feeling very much different than I ever did. I felt I was doing what I could about what was wrong with me, so I felt a little better about that, but generally my state of mind was the same."

"Did you have any discussions with Dr. Hartogs up until June, 1969, concerning the progress that you felt you were making?"

"Dr. Hartogs thought I was making progress based on the fact that I could touch him, that we were touching each other. I was able to take my dress off." She paused for a moment, then said, "I remember one discussion I had with Dr. Hartogs, perhaps in May, when I suggested we talk about the possibility of my seeing a different therapist, a woman therapist. Dr. Hartogs' constant reference to sex was making me uncomfortable. I thought I could speak more openly with a woman."

A small voice inside her kept saying that she was not benefiting from his guidance, no matter how often he said she was getting better. She was astute enough to know the truth, but lacked the courage to act on it, as she had lacked courage so much of her life. She was still being the good little girl who did not make waves. And she could not believe that her psychiatrist could be in the wrong. When she suggested a woman therapist, he said that, considering her "condition," the worst thing she could do was to see a woman—that if he couldn't "cure" her, nobody could.

Yet she still felt depressed much of the time, she was not losing any weight, food was more of a pleasure than being size nine.

He was still saying, every session, "Let's have sex," and she would insist, "I'm not here to have sex. I don't want sex."

Cohen was saying, "Did there come a time when you would both lie on the couch completely nude?"

"Yes," she said.

"Would both of you touch and fondle each other?"

"Yes."

"What did you discuss during these sessions when you were lying on the couch naked with Dr. Hartogs?"

"We discussed my readiness to do this. I didn't want to. I was squeamish about touching him. He said I had to overcome that, that it was not the normal way to be, that I had to learn to be with a man. I had to be able to touch him and not feel uncomfortable about it."

Cohen asked, "Julie, did you have any discussions with Dr. Hartogs up until June, 1969, about the emotional problems for which you went to see him?"

"We discussed it a little bit, not very much. He didn't really want to discuss anything."

Halpern rose to object. "I ask that the latter be stricken."

Judge Myers said, "That will be stricken. The jury will disregard it. The answer to that question is, 'No, he didn't discuss it much.' "

She spoke of her family occasionally, though she sensed he was not very much interested in her childhood. But there were times she felt he was tolerant, listening to her describe her unhappy life. His answers to her questions were, however, usually terse and followed by, "Next question."

Once he said, "I'm going to tell you the start of a story and you finish it in your own words."

"I'm no good at that," she said, thinking of all the English tests she had flunked.

He disregarded her protest. "You are standing at the edge of a grave, looking in. Now go on with the story."

She was silent.

He said encouragingly, "Say anything that enters your mind."

She thought for a minute, said, "I fell in the grave and they covered me up."

Now there was silence on his part. Then he said, "There has to be more than that."

"I can't think of anything else," she said.

Another time she told him, "Someone at *Esquire*

sent me an anonymous note saying, 'Why do you always wear the same dress? I'm sick of looking at it. Get another, for heaven's sake.' "

He looked at her sympathetically, she thought, so she went on, "I was furious. I could never do anything so cruel to someone else."

"What did you do?" he asked.

"I showed the note to the girl who works next to me. She thought it was nasty and underhanded."

He said, "That dress *is* something of a *schmata*."

"What does that mean?" she asked. He was smiling, so she thought he was teasing her.

"That's 'rag' in Yiddish," he said.

She continued to wear the dress, to the office and to her therapy sessions.

Once in a while he asked her to tell him her dreams. In the telling, she thought, dreams lost their feeling of terror, but she did as he requested.

She remembered two particularly frightening dreams. In one, she was looking into a mirror but could see no reflection of herself. Just vague, cloudy outlines. When she woke from this dream, she was crying and so weak she could hardly move.

In the second dream, she was playing her piano. Suddenly the ivory of the keys turned transparent, and she could see the skeleton of the wood underneath. Again she woke up crying and terrified.

She described these two nightmares, not understanding why they should be nightmares at all. Considered in the daytime, there was nothing really scarey about them, but she knew they were two of the worst dreams she'd ever had.

He gave no interpretations. She wondered why he had asked about them.

Because she had so much difficulty relating fantasies about him, which he kept asking for, and remembering her feelings about the people to whom she had been close, he suggested that he inject her with a drug that would cause her to lose consciousness, then a second drug, after which she would regain consciousness to a level where she could speak more freely.

"Absolutely not!" She believed if she were to give up her consciousness, whether through hypnosis or drugs, she had to know and trust the person she was with. She did not trust him completely since he had made sexual suggestions, and she couldn't see herself lying on his couch unconscious—that would be asking for trouble.

She did request his advice about one problem. Chris, who had gone back to Chicago to live for a while, had telephoned, saying she would be in New York for a few days, and asked if she could stay with Julie. Clearly this would involve more than just a house guest camping out in the living room. It was practically certain she and Chris would resume sleeping with each other as lovers. But with what consequences?

About a year ago, when Chris was still living in New York, Julie had been at her desk at *Esquire* when the phone rang. It was Chris, and she sounded dazed.

"What's the matter, Chris?" she asked.

"I've just swallowed all my sleeping pills. I don't want to live," Chris said. "Will you take care of my cat?"

"Where are you?" She felt guilty, since she had been the one to suggest Chris and she break up.

"My phone's out of order. I'm calling from a booth

on the corner. I'm going back to the apartment and die." Chris hung up.

Julie left the office at once and took a cab to Chris's apartment. She raced up the three flights of stairs, banged on the door. There was no response. The door was locked but she pushed hard and the rotted wood gave way.

She heard the stereo blaring jazz, saw Chris stretched out as though dead on the slipcovered couch. Julie turned the stereo off and stood for a moment, conflicted. She thought, Chris has made her choice, maybe I should just leave; then she thought, Chris called to tell me what she had done, so she must have wanted to live, I'd better call an ambulance. She knew of a Catholic hospital in the vicinity, and she looked up the number in the telephone directory. Then she realized Chris's telephone didn't work, so she ran down the three flights to the booth on the corner.

When she got back to Chris's room she tried to wake her by slapping her face, but Chris lay as though lifeless. Julie waited what seemed an hour, still no ambulance, so she ran to the phone booth again. Finally an ambulance arrived and two interns put Chris on a stretcher. Julie rode in the ambulance to the emergency room of the hospital, where they pumped Chris's stomach and inserted a needle attached to a tube into her arm. An intern told Julie they could not tell yet whether Chris would live or die.

Julie walked beside them as they wheeled Chris into a room. They handled her so carelessly that if Julie had not caught Chris's head, it would have cracked into the sharp corner of a table as they lifted her from the stretcher onto the bed. Julie noticed too that the needle in her arm was coming untaped.

Chris needed more care than she seemed to be getting in this place. Julie stayed, dozing in a chair beside Chris's bed. When she woke in the morning, she found Chris could talk groggily. Julie told her she was going home to take a shower but would be back. She returned, bringing Chris toothpaste, a novel, and a goldfish in a bowl, thinking that if Chris saw something lively moving around, she might want to live.

Julie wanted to call Chris's parents and tell them what had happened but Chris asked her not to. Julie thought Chris's attempted suicide had been a way of inducing her to come back.

Now, as she faced Dr. Hartogs, she wondered what would come from resuming her sexual relationship with Chris. There had been no progress that she could see in therapy, but if there were, she didn't want to negate it.

"What shall I do?" she asked.

He said, "By all means she should stay with you."

"You think so?"

"Could I come and stay too?"

A joke, obviously, she thought, an attempt to keep things light. She ignored his remark.

He said, "Many psychiatrists like to see where their patients live. The paintings and books they choose are very revealing."

It was one thing to reveal yourself through conversation, but to stand around helpless while your surroundings told everything didn't sound like a good idea. Besides, she didn't care much for her apartment. She had chosen it mainly because it was within walking distance of her job. It was a typical New York studio apartment, built in the sixties, a white box completely devoid of architectural charm.

Except for the piano and stereo, she had either made or scavenged the few furnishings. The *objets d'art* were a collection of shells, a little brass bird, and an etching, done by Anne, of a chicken sitting on a cracked egg. There were lots of records and quite a few books, many children's stories. She'd covered the couch and made Roman shades for the windows using red, orange, and magenta cotton fabric. These brilliant colors did not at all reflect the way she felt, which was probably the reason she chose them.

She didn't think Dr. Hartogs would learn much about the inside of her head from seeing where she lived. But even if he could, she didn't want him there.

Chris came. They spent a sexually exciting, emotionally devastating week.

Cohen was asking if anything had occurred in July, 1969, in connection with her lying on the couch naked. "Did you begin to have sex with him?"

"No, not yet," she said. "I still resisted having sex with him. I didn't think this was going to do me any good. I remember a discussion I had with Dr. Hartogs about this, trying to explain to him that I felt that I would get hurt in a relationship like this. He assured me I would not get hurt. He promised nothing would happen to hurt me."

"Julie, in July, 1969, did you contemplate suicide?" Cohen asked.

"Yes. . . ."

*　　*　　*

She sat in the chair opposite him and all she could do was cry. It was July, a wicked month in her life. Her father had left her forever in July, and her brother had killed himself in July.

In previous sessions she had tried to talk about her brother, the only man in her life she felt had ever cared for her. But after all, how much could you say in ten minutes? She would just start to remember, burst into tears, and the session was over. When she got to the foot of the stairs she would huddle in her secret hiding place and cry.

In the past twenty-four hours she had worked out the details of a suicide plan in her mind. She called Dr. Hartogs, and he must have sensed her panic, for he gave her a special appointment.

Now she told him, "I've made up my mind to commit suicide."

"What are you saying?" he asked.

"I've quit my job and taken all my money out of the bank," she said. "I'm going to buy a ticket to the Grand Canyon and jump in. No one will ever find my body."

"Where is the money?" he asked.

"Right here." She indicated her purse.

"Give it to me," he said.

Reluctantly she handed him almost $1,000. He gave her another special appointment for the next day. By her next session she no longer felt like killing herself, in part because she thought that at least he cared enough for her to want to stop her from taking her life. He handed her back the almost $1,000.

3

Cohen was asking if she began having sex with Dr. Hartogs after July of 1969.

"Yes," she said, "it was in August. . . ."

The dog days of August enveloped the city. Dr. Hartogs did not take a vacation, but would go to his summer home on Long Island on Sunday afternoons after seeing patients.

She noted every appointment with him on the blue pages of her red leather engagement book. There were four days to a page and she wrote down every appointment with her psychiatrist, her piano teacher, her dentist, and her doctor. Though she put "Dr." in front of the dentist's and doctor's names, she marked appointments with Dr. Hartogs with his initials only. She did not want anyone who might see the diary to know she was going to a psychiatrist.

She made a large circle around the initials "R.H." on Sunday, August 10, at 8 A.M. On that day, she had decided, she would have sex with him.

She felt like some sort of trophy he deserved for his six-month pursuit of her. Maybe he was right, she had to have sex with him if she ever was to have a successful relationship with a man. And it would be something new in her life to have sex with a doctor who said it was for her own good.

When she walked in on Sunday he suggested routinely, "Let's have sex."

"O.K.," she said, "why don't we?"

He looked at her, surprised. "Do you mean it?"

"Let's get it over with," she said.

"I can't," he said. "There are patients in the waiting room."

Now she was surprised. "But there are always patients in the waiting room when you ask me to have sex."

"Come Tuesday night at nine-forty-five," he said. "We'll have more time."

"That seems very late," she said dubiously.

"I'll take you home," he said.

"O.K.," she agreed. Not only would she have sex with her psychiatrist, but he would escort her home afterward, as a suitor would.

That Tuesday night, August 12, she wore one of the new Marimekkos, the skirt black and white, the top all black, with long sleeves.

She was his last patient of the evening. Not a word was said, as though they both understood she had made a bargain and would keep it. He undressed, then helped her take off her new dress.

After they lay down on the couch, naked, he kissed her on the lips, caressed her breasts, then was inside her. She felt him moving, found it difficult to respond. In a few minutes it was over. It was completely unlike any other sexual experience she had known, usually the man had been loving and tender in his lovemaking, never leaving her this way, incomplete.

As she lay stunned, he jumped up, went into the bathroom. She heard the sound of water splashing. She thought he would return and really make love to her. There was plenty of time, since no patient waited.

When he came back, he got dressed. Then, to her astonishment, he went over to the typewriter and began to type. She realized she could expect no more lovemaking, so she got up, went into the bathroom, and took a shower. Then she got dressed and came out.

He looked up from his typing. "Do you mind if I don't take you home?" he said. "I've got a lot of writing to do."

She supposed he was writing a new book or his monthly column for *Cosmopolitan*, "The Analyst's Couch." She felt disappointed but said, "O.K.," not wanting to make demands on this busy, important man.

From force of habit, she gave him the check for $10. He accepted it, saying, "I'll be away over the weekend but I'll see you next Monday night at nine."

The lovemaking, she thought, if you could call it that, had consumed the same amount of time as her regular session—ten minutes.

Cohen was asking, "Thereafter, during your regular visits, did you generally have sexual intercourse with Dr. Hartogs during your regular Thursday and Sunday visits?"

"Generally, yes," she said, "but not every single time."

"After the first time, did you have any conversations concerning the fact that you had sexual intercourse?"

"Dr. Hartogs was pleased that I had finally agreed to have sex with him. He thought this indicated progress on my part. He thought it indicated that I was not a totally homosexual woman. I was happy about that. He

said he didn't know why I had taken so long to come
around to this way of thinking. . . ."

She now had regular appointments, which gave her
a sense of feeling anchored. On Thursday night at ten
o'clock she was the final patient, and on Sunday morning at eight, the first. This meant she no longer saw
the waiting room filled with other patients. At times she
tried to tell him of her problems, her feelings, but he
seemed to want to limit her verbalizing. Only the sex
seemed important to him, and she thought, This must
be the way he does therapy.

At one session he said, "Do you want a quickie?"

"What's a quickie?" she asked, wondering what
could be quicker than their usual sexual session.

"We only have five minutes today. I have a lot of
patients waiting."

"That disgusts me," she said.

He shuffled papers on his desk, said nothing.

She stood up and left.

He would greet her each time with "Hello, darling."
In his accent, it came out "dahlink."

She said, "I don't like you calling me that. Why don't
you call me Julie?"

He didn't answer.

She thought that possibly calling all women darling
saved him from having to remember their names.

She felt funny calling him "Dr. Hartogs." She asked,
"What should I call you?"

"Call me René," he said, "if you want to."

But she never called him anything.

She did say, "I love you," as they lay on the couch.

"Thank you," he said. She wished he had said nothing.

She did not have orgasms with him, which was unusual for her. But she found it impossible with him because she felt no tenderness, no warmth in his touch. He never asked whether she had an orgasm, never showed the slightest interest in the way she felt. She could not repress her rage about her sexual frustration, no matter how hard she tried.

One session he talked about getting some gifts for relatives.

She said, "Your book is on the junk table at Marboro's. You can probably pick up some at fifty cents each to give your relatives."

He was angry. "Why are you so nasty?"

After she left, she crept under the stairs and cried.

When she sat opposite him at the desk, he often interrupted her to take telephone calls. Patients could reach him at any hour, just as she did when she first called for an appointment. After he hung up he never remembered her train of thought but looked at her as though to ask, Were you saying something?

"I have to take care of my business," he said to her once as he reached for the ringing phone.

When he hung up, she said, "You called it your *business*. Don't you mean *practice*?"

"It's a business," he said.

She thought that might have been one of the most honest statements he ever made.

Now that they were on the couch every appointment, he would let the phone ring three times, after which a service would pick it up.

There was a box on his desk with a button that he

pushed to let in patients downstairs at the front door. The box had an extension cord so he could lift it and put it on the floor next to the couch. There would come a click when a patient buzzed, he would reach over and push the button. This would take only a second. But she felt the distraction to be a chain on his time. The knowledge that still another patient was waiting for him would make her feel rushed.

She was aware she was feeling residual anger from the previous Thursday night when, one Sunday morning, she walked in to find him dressed to go to the beach, in shorts and a fishnet shirt. She wanted him to ask her to go along, but he did not. He was wearing sunglasses with magenta rims.

"How do you like my sunglasses?" he asked.

"They're absurd for a man," she said.

He seemed hurt. "You don't like them?"

"No. They're ridiculous," she said.

"You're spiteful," he said, and started to arrange papers on his desk.

"I didn't mean it." Tears came to her eyes.

He was silent.

"Please forgive me," she begged. "I'm sorry I was so nasty. I won't do it again. Just talk to me."

"I really have to go now," he said.

They continued the sexual relationship, but still she could not reach orgasm. She sensed he performed without love. Sometimes his kiss was intense, usually until she responded, then he would pull away and she would have to be the aggressive one if she wanted another kiss. He never kissed her during sex.

She tried to talk to him about the way she felt, saying, "There's something wrong with our lovemaking."

He did not answer.

One time she was driven out of desperation to say, "Are you going to buy the latest Masters and Johnson book?" It was called *Human Sexual Inadequacy*.

"Do you want to find out how sexually inadequate I am?" he asked.

She thought, Maybe he knows he is sexually inadequate and doesn't want me to find substantiation in a book.

She thought one reason for her lack of fulfillment was that she felt so inhibited during the sexual act. He warned her not to make any noise, he didn't want the patients in the waiting room or the tenants above to hear a sound. Once he asked her not to take a bath, afraid patients might overhear. It all made her shrink into herself instead of feeling free.

He asked her to write him letters describing her feelings for him, since, he said, she had trouble verbalizing them. She wrote about once a week saying she loved him, trying, as always, to please him.

He typed a note to her saying, "I love you." He did not sign his name; instead he typed, "Your affectionate rabbit."

Cohen asked if she ever told Dr. Hartogs of her feelings about paying him for each session after having sexual intercourse.

She recalled, "It was probably in September of 1969...."

As he was getting into his trousers she lay on the couch feeling like a dirty dishrag. "I don't like paying a man to have sex with me," she said. "I feel like a prostitute."

"I don't give you money, so you're not a prostitute," he said.

"But I give *you* money," she said. "It's bothering me that I pay you for sex. Don't you think you should stop charging me?"

"I spent a lot of time and money on my education and I work hard in this office to earn money," he said. "Besides, it's part of therapy that the patient has to pay."

"O.K.," she said.

But it bothered her more as time passed.

In November she brought up the matter again. She expected him to be furious, but to her surprise he said, "You don't have to pay any more. I don't need your money."

She felt relieved. But why had he changed his mind? Maybe he was enjoying himself sexually with her; she really did not think he was giving up the money because he was a good Samaritan.

Cohen was asking, "Can you tell us, Julie, other than sexual intercourse, did any other sex acts occur between you and Dr. Hartogs?"

"He would often ask me to kiss his penis. I didn't want to do this. He said this was a normal thing between men and women when they made love, and that I should try to do it. I did this and he did the same thing to me. . . ."

She thought she was overcoming some of her inhibitions. One day she dared ask, "What do three people do together when they have sex?"

"Would you like me to arrange something for us with another person?" he asked.

"No!" she said, horrified. Having sex with him was as daring as she could be.

Once he picked up an electric vibrator from his desk and asked, "Do you know what this is?"

She wasn't sure and didn't want to guess.

He turned it on. "I use it for my face," he said, and illustrated. Then he asked, "Do you want to try it?"

"No," she said. She was embarrassed by her thoughts; it did not look like an innocent gadget.

He stocked the refrigerator full of diet sodas and chocolate-chip cookies. Once she found it stuffed with twenty-five or thirty boxes of cookies, and wondered if he kept them as an antidote for frustrated patients. The refrigerator became one of her favorite retreats after particularly unsatisfying sexual episodes with him.

Cohen was asking if any occasion arose when Dr. Hartogs suggested sexual intercourse but she felt differently about it.

"Yes. . . ."

One Thursday night as they lay on the couch, she felt depressed, unable to respond. She looked up at him apathetically.

He suddenly took her right hand and bent two fingers back, causing such pain that she screamed. Her first thought was that she might not be able to play the piano.

She rubbed her aching fingers, whispering, "You hurt me."

"The pain will go away," he said.

One of the fingers hurt for a week; the other hurt for months.

Another time she did not feel like sex and started to turn away. He pulled her legs apart, got on top of her, forced himself inside.

She did not resist, just lay limply under him. She endured for a minute what was excruciating pain, then screamed.

He put his hand over her mouth. "Don't do that!"

She expected him to comfort her. Instead, he kept his hand over her mouth. She trembled, realizing that other patients might have heard her, and looked at him piteously.

He took his hand away and started getting dressed. "Don't you think you owe me an explanation?" he said.

She felt she did not owe him anything. She stood up, put on her panties, bra, and dress, thinking, We are quarreling but this is not a lover's quarrel where it's fun to make up, this is more the quarrel of enemies.

Cohen asked Julie, "Did there come a time when Dr. Hartogs asked you to do some typing for him?"

"Yes," she said.

"Can you tell us when that occurred and exactly what happened?"

"It was in December of 1969. Dr. Hartogs asked me if I would like to help him with some of his work. At first I told him no, because I thought the terminology would be too complicated. He said it would be very easy, just typing some form letters for him. He explained these were letters that boys had him do, because they didn't want to go to Vietnam, and they needed a doctor's recommendation that they couldn't go. These letters were all the same, with the exception of a couple of words. So, I typed them and he paid me for them."

"Over what period of time did you type these letters, Julie?"

"For about ten months, beginning in December of 1969."

"Did you have an agreed-upon rate of compensation?"

"Yes, he paid me three dollars for each letter I typed."

"Do you recall approximately how many you typed?"

"Hundreds, I don't recall how many."

"Do you recall the contents of these letters?"

Halpern objected, and the judge sustained the objection. But the judge asked the jurors to leave the courtroom, and after they did, he asked Julie, "What was the purpose of the letters?"

She replied, "So that the boys wouldn't have to go to Vietnam. . . ."

Now on Sundays, after her regular appointment, usually after sex, she would type in the library until he finished with the morning patients. The letters were easy, and she was glad to have the work because she was saving money to buy a grand piano. For lunch they would have cold cuts and cookies from the refrigerator, or salads from a local delicatessen. Then they might have sex again. Afterward he would write his column for *Cosmopolitan* or work on an article or book as she resumed typing. Usually she typed the draft letters on his stationery, the letterhead identifying him professionally as doing "Psychotherapy, Psychiatry, and Psy-

choanalysis." Once she retyped his *Cosmopolitan* column after he corrected his first draft. One afternoon he
asked her to have sex for the third time when she had
finished the typing. He would often ask if she did not
feel much better than before, if she wasn't happy to be
having sex with a man rather than a woman, and she
would say yes. She liked the feeling of being close to
someone.

She decided she would give up expecting any show
of love or tenderness from him, that she would act as
he did, divorced from feelings of affection. She would
try to savor only the physical experience. Her new attitude worked; she found she could have an orgasm.

It worked for her body, she thought, but it wasn't doing anything for her head.

At least she felt needed—not loved, but needed. She
thought there was nothing personal about his need for
her, any woman would do. She believed there were
other women in his life—there must be if this was his
way of treating lesbians, for she could not be the only
patient with this problem.

Just after Christmas she thought she had symptoms
of a vaginal infection and made an appointment to see
her regular doctor. He examined her, told her she had
a highly contagious infection called trichomoniasis,
transmitted by a man from woman to woman. She felt
embarrassed to have her doctor discover she had such
a disease.

To get rid of it, her doctor said, both she and the
gentleman she was involved with had to take the same
medication. He wrote her a prescription for pills called
Flagyl.

Julie gave Dr. Hartogs half the pills and explained he would have to take them. He agreed to do so.

Four months later, she still had the infection, so she went again to see her doctor.

"You haven't got rid of the trichomoniasis, Julie. Make sure you and the gentleman both take the pills," he warned her.

She asked him to give her a prescription for half the original amount, as the pills were expensive. She explained the "gentleman" was a doctor and could get his own.

She felt angry at Dr. Hartogs. She had faithfully taken her pills, and was sure he had neglected taking his, since the infection didn't affect his body. He might well be having sex with another woman who was, through him, infecting her, she thought.

When she saw him three days later, a Sunday, she told him she still had the infection and asked if he was taking his pills. He said yes. She asked to see them.

"I left them home," he said.

"I don't believe you," she said. "You're not taking them." She added angrily, "I'll have this disease forever if you won't help me get over it."

He wrote out a prescription in her name. "Get this filled for me," he said, handing her some money. "I'll keep the bottle here and take the pills regularly."

She went the same day to Clyde Chemists and had the prescription filled. Weeks later the infection finally cleared up.

Sometimes when he was not besieged by other patients, he gave her a long session, twenty minutes, usually for sex. There were times they did not have sex. One Thursday night he told her as she walked in, "I have to see a patient after you, so we can't have sex tonight."

Nobody had ever followed her on a Thursday and she felt upset. As she walked down the stairs, she saw, standing in the lobby waiting for the elevator, a young woman exquisitely groomed, wearing a pink coat. Julie thought perhaps this woman was not his patient, that she might be going to another floor. She watched the woman step on the elevator, then noted with despair that the elevator stopped at the second floor.

She felt a tearing jealousy, more intense than she had ever experienced before. She could not breathe. She could not cry. It was as though all emotion had drained out of her.

Somehow she got home. She ran to the shower and, without taking off her clothes, turned on the cold water and stood under it. The cool drenching helped ease her.

At her next appointment she asked why he had seen the woman in the pink coat. He said she was a former patient who had suicidal impulses and had called for help.

This episode forced her to face the fact that her entire emotional life depended on him. It wasn't as if she had a boy friend *and* a psychiatrist—her psychiatrist was the only source of her self-esteem. It was pathetic, she thought; her emotional age had never caught up with her chronological one. She felt unsophisticated, like a child; people always took her for younger than she was.

She also had the feeling, and it was growing stronger, that she wasn't getting better. When she tried to tell him she still felt depressed, he would shuffle papers on his desk, or go to the typewriter, or open a book, or walk around the room. She knew a psychiatrist was not supposed to act like that.

And yet he made her feel special. She had always been self-conscious about her body but he seemed to like it. He told her he did not admire skinny, sticklike women, and at the moment this was more important to her than the fact that he did not seem interested in her problems.

She sensed he was grateful if she didn't cry or complain about her petty life. She thought, This important man is all talked out, or rather listened out, by the end of the day; he is making it quite clear I would be doing him a favor if I kept quiet.

He told her one Thursday that he had fallen asleep with the patient before her.

"What happened?" she asked.

"He just kept talking."

"How do you know if you were asleep?"

"I know," he said. "They always talk."

She certainly was not going to inflict any more chatter on him.

She would have liked to see more of him but he worked from seven in the morning until eleven at night. He saw what he described as "heaps of patients"; his appointment book did not reflect all the appointments. It was indeed a business, she thought.

One Sunday morning the buzzer to the downstairs door clicked as they were having sex. He made no move toward the box on the floor to let the patient in.

"Somebody's here very early," she said.

"I'll just ignore it," he said.

The buzzer kept sounding, as if someone were anxious to get in. She thought, That's not a man, no man would keep buzzing so insistently, it's got to be a desperate woman, perhaps one who once had this hour.

After about ten minutes the buzzer stopped ringing. A second later the bell at the door outside the waiting room started to ring. Another tenant must have let the woman in downstairs.

They were dressed by this time. Dr. Hartogs went to the front door and peered through the little opening.

He came back. "This crazy woman," he said. "She's an alcoholic. She's always bothering me."

Julie was aghast. How could a psychiatrist call a patient "crazy"? He was supposed to understand her illness, not speak of her with contempt.

He said, "I'll let her in and you leave as if your session were just over."

She managed to look at the woman in passing. She was a young girl carrying a flower in her hand. The girl's face was stricken and weary, as if she had been up all night, and she was crying.

She thought, O.K., Julie, there you are in about a year.

4

~~~~~~~~~~~~~~~~~~~~~~~~~~~~~~~~

Cohen was asking if she saw Dr. Hartogs other than in his office during 1970.

"Yes. . . ."

This year, for a change, July proved a happy month. Dr. Hartogs moved from the west side of the city to a small one-bedroom apartment near his office. She did not know whether he was moving because he was divorcing or being divorced. She never asked him about his personal life, nor did he say much about it.

One Thursday night she helped him carry shopping bags full of magazines and books from his office to the apartment. In the bedroom she saw a light-green antique bed, shaped like a sleigh, and covered with decals. There were no rugs on the floors, and not much furniture.

He asked her to stay overnight. It was the first time she had slept with him in a bed and she was overjoyed at this new intimacy.

When he asked what she thought of the paintings on his wall, many of which he had done, she felt embarrassed. Most of them were without composition or clear content, just gigantic splashes of color, and she thought them laughable. She said nothing, pretending to be amused by his titles. He called one, depicting three blind boatmen on a gondola, "Venetian Blinds."

Another was an unsensual nude, with one large breast constructed of an automobile taillight that plugged into a wall socket and lit up.

Several evenings he asked her to the apartment, and she had him to herself for at least eight hours. For him to want her close all night, to eat at his dining table, to share a home even for a short time, seemed to indicate that she was part of his life now.

She was concerned about his health, afraid he was working too hard and not eating properly, what with the macaroni and potato salads from the delicatessen and the chocolate-chip cookies and diet sodas from his refrigerator. One Thursday she brought him a chicken she had broiled, seasoned with lemon and vermouth, and he ate it with pleasure.

When she stayed over, sometimes she worried because she could not hear him breathing at night. She would listen, afraid he might have had a heart attack, and shake him. He would then snore gently, as though informing her he was still alive.

She did not sleep well those nights, and would be groggy at her job the next morning, even after a shower. But, she thought, she had all week to catch up on sleep.

In spite of the new closeness between them, she felt she was never the first thing on his mind; he seemed to be thinking of other things even as he spoke to her. But she was honored he thought of her at all. She believed he did not know how to relate in a romantic way to women, that any man who worked sixteen hours a day probably would have the same difficulty—but this was just a guess. She did not have much experience

with friends, lovers, or therapists, much less a man
who claimed to be all three.

Judge Myers was questioning her now. "How many
times did you visit his apartment?"

"Perhaps five times in all," she said.

"Can you tell us whether you had sex with him on
each occasion?" Cohen asked.

"Yes, I did," she said.

"What did the sex act consist of?"

"It always consisted of intercourse. It didn't always
consist of the other thing I mentioned." She was referring to oral sex.

The judge asked, "Did it, at any time, consist of the
other thing you mentioned?"

"Yes," she said.

Cohen asked, "Did you have any conversations with
Dr. Hartogs in 1970, before your therapy with him
terminated, about your progress?"

"Dr. Hartogs thought I was making progress. He
thought the evidence was that I was able to have sexual
contact with him. I thought I was making progress at
that time, too. . . ."

At times he shared his problems with her and she
was flattered. One day he told her he had canceled all
his appointments and was going to a hospital to have
his face lifted. She did not understand why he wanted
to do this; his chin was not flabby.

He told her he would be in the hospital three or four
days, and planned to drive there and back.

"You might not be feeling well when you get out,"
she said. "Let me take you home."

He declined her offer.

"What are you telling patients?" she asked.

"That I've been in an automobile accident," he said.

Then he changed his mind, decided not to have the operation; she never knew why.

Judge Myers declared a recess for lunch. The jury filed out and the judge left the room, as did all the spectators.

She walked over to the counsel table, eager to find out how she had done.

Bob was smiling. "You were great," he said.

Loren too looked pleased. "Want lunch?" he asked.

Julie did not feel like eating or drinking. For once something was more important to her than food: her testimony.

Loren picked up a light lunch, brought it back, and joined Julie and Bob in preparing for the afternoon session.

When court reconvened at two o'clock, Julie resumed her place in the witness chair. Cohen asked whether she could recall any conversations she had in 1970 with Dr. Hartogs concerning her emotional problems.

"Yes," she said. "In the winter. I would ask Dr. Hartogs if I could talk to him about some things that were bothering me. He would tell me that the talking was not the essential part of the therapy. He insisted we have sex and that whatever was bothering me wouldn't be bothering me much longer."

Cohen asked, "From January of 1970 until July of 1970, you continued to see Dr. Hartogs twice a week at his office, is that correct?"

"Yes," she said.

"Did you reach a decision at any time during the summer of 1970 to attempt to terminate the therapy you were receiving from Dr. Hartogs?"

"Yes. . . ."

As August approached, he spent Sunday afternoons at his home on Long Island, as he had done the year before. She longed to be with him but he never asked her. Even on nights they spent together in his bed, he seemed just as distant as he had been in the office after sex, only she was more disappointed because she had expected greater closeness.

He told her he was going to Holland for a week. She thought how exciting it would be to travel with him, and told him she would like to go.

"I can't take you," he said. "I have to see relatives. It wouldn't look right if I arrived with a young woman."

She thought all his relatives had died in a concentration camp; that's what he'd told her. Well, she thought, maybe a great-uncle or great-aunt had survived. She consoled herself with the thought this might be an occasion for him to bring her a present.

She suddenly wanted to talk to someone about their involvement, perhaps to feel less lonely while he was away. She asked, "Do you mind if I tell Anne about us?"

"Do you have a confession compulsion?" he said.

She was not sure what the term meant, but his tone told her he did not approve of the idea.

He added, "I'd rather you didn't say anything about our relationship to anyone."

So she suffered in silence, missing him deeply.

After his return she went gaily to his office, expecting he would be very happy to see her. To her chagrin, she found the waiting room as crowded as the first day she entered. It was clear they would not be spending much time together, five minutes at the most.

As she walked into his office, he acted as though he had never been away. He said, as he always did, "How are you, darling?" He made no gesture toward her, showed no sign they had ever been intimate.

She asked, "Did you bring me anything?"

"No," he said. "What did you expect me to bring you?"

She was crestfallen. Obviously he had not thought about her all the time he was away, whereas she constantly had been on her mind.

There was, of course, no time for sex.

When she left, she again hid under the stairs, crying quietly, holding her breath so she would not make a noise. She had not done this in a long time.

She was sure he would give her something for her birthday; she had told him it was September 8. But when she walked into his office that Thursday, there was no gift, no card, no birthday greeting.

She rebuked him. "You forgot my birthday."

"I've had so many things on my mind," he said.

She felt hurt, but then he was a very busy man. What right did she have to think he would take the time to buy her a gift, or even a card? Birthday celebrations were for children.

They walked to his apartment to spend the night. She admired the light-green sheets, which matched the decaled bed.

"I'll get you green sheets for your birthday," he said.

She flipped over the top sheet, then noticed a large stain on the bottom sheet. She was shocked.

"You'll have to change these sheets," she said.

He said, "The maid forgot to change them."

"If there were dirty dishes in the sink I wouldn't mind," she said angrily. "But this stain shows some other woman has been here."

"You mean if you saw a woman's umbrella in the apartment you'd think she'd been in bed with me?" he said.

"An umbrella is not the same as a dirty stain on the bed."

They had sex, but this time it was different. She had always tried to ignore the possibility there were other women in his life, but the stained sheet could not be ignored.

She realized their relationship would not improve. She could never expect him to cure her depressions; all she could look forward to was existing in the same way, month after month, seeing him when *he* wanted to see *her,* obeying all his commands like a good little slave.

She had felt suspended, put on a shelf, for most of the month of August. Now, even in September, he sometimes took Sundays off, asked her to come Saturday mornings instead, then after sex would give her letters to type, and leave for Long Island.

One Saturday morning she told him, "I'm not going to see you again. I'm as depressed as ever. I haven't changed at all." It happened spontaneously; she had not consciously made up her mind to say it.

The episode of the stained sheet still haunted her, but

more than that, his forgetting her birthday wounded
her. Somehow this was an echo of all the birthdays in
her life when her absent father once again forgot.

"There's no time to talk about it now," he said. "Can
I call you at home this afternoon?"

"O.K.," she said, surprised. He seldom called her at
home.

She waited by the phone the rest of the day. It rang
at five. He asked what was bothering her.

"I really don't want to see you anymore," she said.
"I'm not getting better."

"I think you are getting better and should continue
to see me," he said.

She was silent.

He said, "May I have dinner with you this evening?"

This was the first time he had made such a formal
request.

"O.K.," she said.

"Come to my apartment about six," he said.

She met him at six and he took her to the Budapest
Restaurant for a Hungarian meal, then to a movie he
selected, Barbra Streisand in *On a Clear Day,* which she
could barely sit through. It was difficult for her to talk
to him, as they had not been in the habit of making
social chitchat. She assumed that her threat to break
off had made him realize how much she meant to him,
that they had finally got off one plateau in the relationship and were climbing to another.

After the movie they went to his apartment and he
put away some of his possessions while she sat in the
living room, looking at a book of paintings by Hierony-
mus Bosch. When they went to bed he set the alarm,

for he was leaving in the morning for Long Island. Once again she felt deserted.

At her next Thursday-night appointment he gave her three letters to type and return to him. Then he said, "I don't know my plans for the weekend. I'll call you Saturday."

She spent the weekend by the telephone, not leaving the apartment. Her fury at him mounted. He had not called by Monday morning, so she decided to go to work.

He called her that morning at *Esquire* and asked her to bring him the three letters at once. She said she could not stop work to take the letters to him. He called again; again she refused to leave her desk. He called a third time; she still refused.

Then he said he would send a messenger for the letters to her apartment during the evening. She went home and waited. At midnight the doorman buzzed and said someone was downstairs waiting for an envelope. Thinking it was the messenger, she said she would bring it down.

As she stepped into the lobby she saw Dr. Hartogs, a look of fury on his face. She wanted to talk to him. But he snatched the envelope and dashed out the door. They exchanged not a word.

The rest of that night, all day Tuesday, and Tuesday night, she was in a deep depression. Wednesday morning, too upset to go to work, she called him and said she was very sorry for the way she had acted. He told her he had stayed up until three in the morning typing letters.

Then he said, "Could you come to the office at three this afternoon?"

"Of course," she said, feeling the first moment of joy in five days.

She thought they would make up that afternoon, but he only asked her to type in the library while he saw patients. He made no sexual advances. When she had finished the letters, he asked her to come Saturday morning at eight, saying they would talk things over then.

She barely got through Thursday and Friday. On Saturday she showed up at his office promptly. She started again to apologize but he seemed not to want to listen. He shoved some letters at her and asked her to type them in the library.

"I want to talk to you," she said.

"I have no time now," he said. "Finish the letters and then we'll talk."

She typed away, tears in her eyes, thinking she would do anything for him if he would just tell her he had forgiven her. She wanted only to be near him again.

When she handed him the letters, he told her, "I don't have time to talk. Patients are waiting. I'll call you tonight."

She went home defeated. She had started to make slight demands on him and he lost interest in her; if she asked for anything she was asking too much. Five minutes after she was no longer available, she thought, there would be another woman to fill his sexual needs. He held all the cards.

He did not call her that night or the next. She was depressed and crying for three days. Then, on the third night, she called him and said she had changed her mind, she thought she needed further therapy and would like to make another appointment.

He said he was too busy.

She told him she was again at the point of considering suicide, she did not know what to do, wouldn't he see her?

"I don't have time," he said.

"Then please recommend another therapist. I have to talk to somebody."

He said he could recommend no one. And he hung up.

She stared at the telephone, the receiver still in her hand. How could he abandon her so abruptly? Did he not hold some small shred of affection for her, after knowing her so intimately for more than a year? It was unbelievable, a man did not do this to a woman with whom he had been sexually close, much less to a patient whom he had urged into a sexual relationship on the grounds it would make her "feel better"—whatever that meant, she thought grimly.

Cohen was asking about the medication Dr. Hartogs had prescribed, including Dexamyl, Triavil, and Elavil. He had before him photostatic copies of the prescriptions, which were part of the court exhibits.

Once she had to go to Chicago on an advertising assignment for *Esquire*. This was exciting but frightening. All the people from *Esquire* would be staying at the Ambassador East, a block away from where she used to live. The trip would certainly be posh compared with the grubby life-style she and Anton endured four years before.

Dr. Hartogs asked why she was afraid, and she told him she always felt insecure in strange surroundings.

There would be so much work to do she could not risk a depression.

He gave her a handful of packets from a big box he kept in the closet. Each packet contained six Dexamyl tablets. He suggested she take one any time she was feeling down, saying, "They'll turn you into a real chatterbox."

Chicago was worse than she'd expected. She just couldn't get caught up in the urgency of the men's fashion business. On the final evening there was a dinner where people got awards for adding half an inch to the width of a lapel, or taking two inches from the length of a jacket. Dexamyl or not, she was deeply depressed.

She checked out of the Ambassador early the next morning and took a cab to the airport. A skycap took her bag and asked, "Where to?"

"San Francisco," she said.

"Flight leaves in forty-five minutes," he said.

There was just enough time to turn in her first-class return ticket to New York. With that money and what was left of the cash she brought with her, she purchased a ticket to San Francisco—one way.

She cried most of the trip to the coast. The stewardesses were sympathetic; they thought she was afraid of flying. She asked them about a place to stay in San Francisco and they gave her directions to an inexpensive hotel near Union Square. It was not fancy, but respectable.

She had no idea why she came or what she was going to do. Not bothering to undress, she lay down on the bed and cried herself to sleep.

In the morning she brushed her teeth, smoothed the

wrinkles out of her clothes, picked up her bag, and left the hotel. Questioning people on the street, she found her way to the airlines terminal, checked her bag, then asked a porter for the address of the nearest pawnshop.

On Market Street, a man quoted a price for her gold earrings and bracelet. She needed more. He added a few dollars but it was still not enough. She snatched up her jewelry and left.

In a second shop she told the man exactly how much she needed—$175, the price of an airline ticket to New York. She explained she couldn't bargain with him because she would not be able to bargain with the man who sold airline tickets. He gave her the money. Her gold earrings and bracelet went into a little brown envelope with her name and a number on it.

She slept most of the trip east. She didn't know why she'd gone to San Francisco, didn't want to know why.

She told Dr. Hartogs the Dexamyl hadn't worked. He said not to worry, they would try something else. Reaching into his box, he gave her several little bottles containing Etrafon, a tranquilizer.

One day in March he surprised her by saying, "I think you should take birth-control pills. I'll write a prescription."

"I don't want to take them," she said.

Then she decided to go to her own doctor and get a prescription. She took the pills even though she really didn't want to; she had heard the side effects could be dangerous.

Dr. Hartogs received many free samples of pills from pharmaceutical companies. Most were tranquilizers. He would give her some, and whenever she could not fall asleep she would take one, though she really did not need pills, she thought; she spent too much time sleeping anyhow.

Cohen was asking, "Did you call any other psychologist or analyst or therapist after your conversation with Dr. Hartogs?"

"Yes. . . ."

Desperate, she called Anne. She was sobbing, hardly able to speak as she told Anne the whole story.

Anne was outraged. "How can someone in his profession behave with so little respect for your suffering?" she said. Anne later told her she had thought, This will be the end of Julie, she will never trust another therapist, and so she will never get better.

Anne wanted her to see Dr. Anderson at once.

"I can't call her," Julie said. She was still angry at Dr. Anderson.

But later she was so distraught she did call Dr. Anderson, who agreed to see her the next day, a Sunday, even though Dr. Anderson never worked on Sunday.

Somehow she got through the night. The next afternoon, in Dr. Anderson's office, between sobs, she described how she had gone to Dr. Hartogs, as Dr. Anderson had suggested nineteen months before, and how they had become sexually involved.

Dr. Anderson looked aghast, but did not question her veracity. She seemed convinced by the intensity of Julie's feelings, her tear-stained face. Dr. Anderson offered to see her twice a week at $10 a session, and she accepted even though she thought of Dr. Anderson as party to the betrayal.

Because she needed money, she decided to continue

typing for Dr. Hartogs. She called him, they set a time for her to come to the office, he handed her letters, she typed them in the library, she went home.

She endured this for two weeks, then decided it was too painful. She could not work so near him and never touch him or be touched by him.

He phoned her at home and asked why she was no longer coming to type. She grasped for an excuse. "I slipped on some ice cream on the sidewalk and fell and fractured my arm."

"Can you type?" he asked.

"No," she said.

"Well, come when you're better," he said.

Week after week with Dr. Anderson she sat crying, sometimes howling in pain, saying over and over, "He said he loved me. He said if I had sex with him I'd get better. And now he won't see me anymore." It was a litany, there was nothing new she could add. She said to Dr. Anderson, "You must be sick of hearing the same thing, but I can't think about anything else. It's taken over my mind."

Only sleep brought escape. She would wake each morning, and in the split second between slumber and consciousness she would think, What is it that's so heavy on my mind? Then the memory of what he had done to her would rush in and drive away all other thoughts for the day.

She told herself how stupid she had been to believe this man. It was not as though she were a young girl, she was thirty years old. She was furious at herself, she had known all along she would get hurt, that he could terminate the relationship at any moment. She raged too because she had felt such deep emotion, whereas he seemed to feel none at all. He could have said, "I'm really sorry you feel this way. It was all a disastrous mistake," but he said nothing, merely hung up the telephone when she asked for help.

She asked Dr. Anderson, "Do you ever see Dr. Hartogs?"

"I see him once in a while at conventions," Dr. Anderson said.

"Don't you say anything to him about what he did?" she asked.

"No," said Dr. Anderson.

"How can you stand it?" she demanded. "How can you not go up to him and say, 'See what you did, you bastard, I sent you this patient and you destroyed her.'"

She felt so angry at Dr. Anderson that one day she threw her gloves at the Afghan dog, knowing she really wanted to hurl them at Dr. Anderson.

No one was going to avenge her, she thought; she would have to do it herself. Dr. Hartogs had destroyed her and she would destroy him, then commit suicide. She planned exactly how—she would shoot him on the street as he left his office late at night.

To try to pull herself out of the depression she had registered for a university course in philosophy. One of the men in her class was a drug dealer; she would arrange to buy a gun from him.

She told Dr. Anderson what she intended to do. Her anger, she explained, was increasing every day, and she could no longer control it.

"I'll have to go to the police and tell them of your threat," said Dr. Anderson.

"I thought what went on in therapy was sacred," she said.

"If you buy a gun, I shall have to tell the police."

So, for the second time, she quit seeing Dr. Anderson. She could not get through the days without crying; she often stayed home from work. Finally she had to tell Evan the truth.

Evan was shocked. "A psychiatrist?" he said.

"Yes."

"He did that?" As though he could not believe it.

She thought he might fire her but, as always, Evan was sympathetic. He said, "If you broke an arm or leg, I wouldn't fire you. This is another kind of sickness."

Cohen was asking, "Did you undertake therapy with other psychiatrists or psychologists?"

"Yes. . . ."

Anne knew only Dr. Anderson, Dr. Hartogs would not refer her to another psychiatrist, so she decided to ask her regular doctor to give her the name of a therapist.

He told her to call Dr. Walter Sencer. She did, and Dr. Senser gave her an appointment. He asked her what psychotherapy she had had, and with whom.

"I've been seeing Dr. Pauline Anderson and before that, I went to a psychiatrist for a year and a half," she said.

Then she told him that sex had been the most important part of the therapy and that now the psychiatrist refused to see her.

Dr. Sencer seemed appalled. He asked, "What's the psychiatrist's name?"

"I can't tell you," she said.

"Why are you protecting him?" he asked. "Look what he's done to you."

Dr. Sencer asked if she would call her former psychiatrist and request a report from him on her treatment. She said she would do this.

Before telephoning Dr. Hartogs, she made notes on what she wanted to say. Then she picked up the telephone. It was January 27, 1971, almost two years after she had first walked into his office.

Obviously there was a patient in his office, as always, but he listened as she told him she was seeing a new psychiatrist, who had asked for a report on her previous treatment.

Dr. Hartogs said, "Don't tell him anything and don't mention any names."

"But I need your report," she said.

"I'll call you back in a day or so," he said and hung up.

He called two days later, on January 29, to ask for a fuller explanation of what she wanted.

She said, "I'm confused about what happened in my therapy with you and thought you could describe it better than I. Will you send Dr. Sencer a report?"

"What should I say?" he asked.

"Say whatever you want. Just describe what happened."

"I couldn't put that in writing," he said.

"Put what in writing?" she asked innocently.

"That we had sex."

"Sex was part of it, so you really should include it," she said. "But I can't tell you what to say."

"What are the dates you came to me?" he asked.

"I don't remember them. You must have them in your

files," she said. She remembered the exact dates but did not want to make it easy for him.

"Could you give me an approximate idea?" he asked.

"No," she said.

"What are you going to tell Dr. Sencer?" he asked.

"I'm going to tell him everything that happened," she said.

"Will you please be discreet and not give my name?" he asked.

"Your name will be on the report you write for him about my treatment," she said. She realized how incriminating that report would be. Then she asked, "Will you also include a list of the medications you prescribed?"

"What medication?" he asked.

"The eight prescriptions, plus various samples of medication you gave me," she said. Dr. Sencer had asked her to get this as well.

"Would you come to the office tonight and bring any empty bottles you have, so I can figure out the medication?" Dr. Hartogs asked.

"No." She did not want to see him. "If you prescribed drugs, you must have records."

"I do," he said. "But I want to check them."

"No," she said firmly. She had been under his spell, sexually and emotionally, long enough.

Then she said, consulting one of the notes she had written, "I'd like my money back. Everything I paid you for therapy. My head is even more messed up as a result of seeing you and it's going to cost a lot to put it together again."

"Your head was a mess when you came to me," he said. "Are you trying to blackmail me?"

"No," she said. "Do you think you did anything that might make you eligible for blackmail? All I'm asking is a report on my therapy and a list of the medications you gave me."

"I'll give you five hundred dollars and additional help, from time to time, if you leave my name out of this," he said.

"I want what I paid you," she said. "But if you consider it blackmail, I won't accept a penny."

"When a surgeon makes a mistake, the patient still pays," he said.

"If you'd been a surgeon, I would certainly be dead. But you aren't and I'm alive, and I want my money back," she said.

"I'll call you back," he said.

He never did.

She went to Dr. Sencer several times, but at $45 an hour could not afford him very long. He suggested she go to the Postgraduate Center for Mental Health, where the fees were smaller. He also investigated the procedure for bringing charges of malpractice against a psychiatrist and gave her the names of a medical board to which she could write.

She drafted a letter, then called the board's headquarters to ask if a psychiatrist could sue a patient for maligning his character should the patient claim sex had been part of the therapy he prescribed. A woman at the other end of the phone said unsympathetically, "If you get involved in something like that, what do you expect? Of course he can sue."

She decided not to send the letter. But spurred on by Dr. Sencer's indignation at what had happened to her, she decided to see what her rights were. In January,

1971, she called the Legal Aid Society of New York and was referred to a lawyer who agreed to handle her case. Then, still not sure she should go ahead with the suit, she decided to check with the only other lawyer she knew, Bob Cohen. She had not consulted Bob since 1966, when he handled her divorce.

She called Bob's office and learned he had left to join another law firm. The telephone operator gave her the firm's name, Lans Feinberg and Cohen, and she phoned him there.

He seemed glad to hear from her. "What's your problem, Julie?" he asked.

"I don't want to bother you about a minor matter," she said.

"Come over and talk about it," he said.

She went to Bob's new office. Bob, who headed the firm's litigation department, was slim, dark-haired, with expressive brown eyes and an easy, confident manner.

As she told him her story, Bob listened carefully, his face showing first amazement, then anger. As she talked she felt humiliated, at times wringing her hands or rocking back and forth, her arms crossing her breasts as though in supplication, her voice so low Bob would have to ask gently, "What did you say, Julie?" Though he looked shocked, he did not add to her load of shame, but was sympathetic.

When she finished, he said, "I don't know too much about psychiatrists, but I have a feeling that what Dr. Hartogs did to you is a violation of the trust requisite to the healing process. I think it constitutes malpractice."

She left it up to Bob to decide what to do; perhaps he could get her money back for her. He introduced her to

Loren Plotkin, a lawyer in his firm who was knowledge-able about psychiatry.

At first Julie was embarrassed that another person should know about her humiliation. But as she listened to Loren answering Bob's questions about the proper relationship between psychiatrist and patient, she felt more at ease. Loren had a friendly manner, and serious brown eyes that often laughed. He was six feet tall, though, as he told her, "I feel six feet one in the sum-mer when I'm relaxed and five feet eleven in the winter when life seems harder." He reminded her of Allan, who had made the bad moments in her life seem better.

Bob and Loren spent over a month deciding what action to take. They interviewed Dr. Sencer for two hours. Though they believed Julie was telling the truth, they wanted an expert's opinion. Dr. Sencer told them he thought she was not hallucinating or having delusions about her sexual experiences with Dr. Hartogs. Dr. Sen-cer also said he thought she showed substantial psycho-logical damage as a result of her so-called therapy.

The first step Bob took was to write Dr. Hartogs a letter on February 11, 1971:

> We have been retained by Miss Julie Roy to institute suit on her claims against you predicated upon, among other things, malpractice, assault and breach of fiduciary duty.
>
> We would be willing on behalf of Miss Roy to confer with you and/or your counsel to discuss the situation. However, we have been instructed not to defer the commencement of litigation beyond Feb-

ruary 25, 1971, unless prior to that time arrangements are made to rectify Miss Roy's grievance.

Five days later Bob received a letter from Dr. Hartogs:

Herewith I wish to inform you, that I have sent to Miss Julie Roy a check in the amount she wants to get.

I wish to stress, that this act does not represent in any way an admission of any guilt, but is merely designed to save her and me the stress and waste of time of any legal procedure as well as to help her to obtain further psychiatric help, which she herself states she needs.

Dr. Hartogs sent her a check for $1,000. She turned it over to Bob, who had written Dr. Hartogs on February 18:

I have your letter of February 16, 1971. According to Miss Roy, the contents are inaccurate. She had not agreed to settle her claim. In the event that you have sent a check I have directed that Miss Roy forward it to me for return to you. In the meantime, if you should like to discuss the matter of settlement I would appreciate if you or your attorney would communicate with me directly.

Bob returned the $1,000 check to Dr. Hartogs on February 19.

Julie was surprised to receive a telephone call from Dr. Hartogs after he got the check back.

"Come in and talk to me about this," he said. "I'm sure we can work everything out."

"I'm through talking to you," she said. "Anything you want to talk over now, talk over with my attorneys. I've said all I have to say to you." This time she was the one to hang up.

The phone rang again immediately. She let it ring.

Meanwhile, Loren's research had turned up no direct precedent for the case. The most common reasons for malpractice suits in the psychiatric profession were fracture from electroshock therapy, suicide of a patient, and erroneous commitment to mental institutions. A few cases arose as a result of what was referred to as "defective psychotherapeutic technique," and a few to drug treatment that might have caused physical damage. Most of the litigation resulted from physical, not psychic, injury to the patient.

A summons and complaint were served on Dr. Hartogs on March 5, 1971, seeking damages of $250,000 on each of five causes of action, totaling $1,250,000. The first two causes of action dealt with his wrongful use of sexual intercourse as therapy, resulting in "irreparable mental and emotional discomfort and harm" to Julie Roy. The other three causes of action dealt with violations of the penal law of the state of New York, charging that because of the use of "transference," which deprived Julie Roy of "informed consent," the sexual intercourse was rape.

Shocked at the amount of damages sought, Julie asked Bob, "Why so much?" She felt she had been mistreated, but put no higher price on her suffering than the money she had given Dr. Hartogs.

"We're suing for malpractice—not for what you

spent," Bob told her. "As a result of what Dr. Hartogs did to you, you're going to have to spend a lot of money to get help. You've already seen Dr. Anderson and Dr. Sencer, and you may see other therapists in the future. Even so, we can't be sure that you'll ever recover from the psychic damage Dr. Hartogs has inflicted on you. The point is, not only did Dr. Hartogs fail to help you, but he worsened your condition a great deal."

He explained the issues involved and the importance of the case—because no patient had ever sued a psychiatrist for malpractice on the grounds he used sex with him as therapy, its decision would be a trail-blazer. She thought that maybe she, who had been treated like dirt by Dr. Hartogs, might have a chance at recovering her self-esteem. She did not think Bob would take the case unless he believed he could win.

She started to feel she wanted the sordid facts made public so other women would be spared her anguish. She suspected Dr. Hartogs had had sex with other women under similar circumstances, and maybe there were other psychiatrists engaged in the same practice who would think twice when they heard of her suit.

The profession needed far better policing of its own, she thought. The public was not well informed, it could not detect the incompetent or unethical members of the mental health field. A patient who was desperate would accept anyone available, as she had done, without questioning.

Few people understood the difference between a psychoanalyst, a psychiatrist, and a psychologist, or realized that no one, not even a psychiatrist, could rightfully call himself a psychoanalyst unless he had received special training in a recognized psychoanalytic institute and had undergone psychoanalysis himself. The public needed to become aware of the lunatic fringe operating as therapists in the mental health field, which attracted men and women who wanted to play God and who were gratified by the patient's fantasy that they were godlike. When it came to therapy, it was, indeed, "Let the buyer beware."

Julie thought that just as a child has to depend on his parents for so many years while his psyche is forming, so does an adult seeking help depend on the therapist. For a regular doctor to have sex with a patient would be a violation of ethics, but for a psychiatrist to do so was a crime of the most devastating nature. It was more than a rape of the body; it was a rape of the mind.

When Anne learned of the suit she told Julie, "It's really a long shot." Then she said, "I'm for it. At least you're getting out your feelings against this man. The worst thing is to feel helpless."

Bob and Loren warned her the suit would take a long time, as was common in the backlogged courts. But she was prepared for a lengthy wait; what else was there in life?

5

As Julie's testimony continued, Cohen asked, "After the Postgraduate Center for Mental Health clinic, to which you had been referred by Dr. Sencer, did you continue psychotherapy there or with anybody else?"

At the Postgraduate Center for Mental Health, where Dr. Sencer had said she might get therapy for $15 an hour, she was interviewed by a psychiatrist who told her he would let her know if she was eligible. While waiting for his decision, she saw Dr. Anderson to keep herself together. She was still crying all the time and thinking seriously of killing Dr. Hartogs and herself.

She informed Dr. Anderson of the malpractice suit and Dr. Anderson advised against it, fearing Julie would be hurt even more. After a few sessions she again stopped seeing Dr. Anderson; she still could not forgive her for originally recommending Dr. Hartogs.

The Postgraduate Center wrote it could not accept her, but listed the names of three senior staff psychiatrists who had office hours for patients referred by the clinic at the same price or only slightly higher than the clinic's. She selected Dr. Barnett Rosenblum, whose office was in the building next to Dr. Hartogs'. She went to Dr. Rosenblum once, on January 29, 1971, paying $25, which she considered expensive compared to the $15 the clinic would have cost. She canceled a second appointment, thinking, I've had enough of psychiatrists.

Several months later, however, on April 14, still depressed, she decided to walk to the Payne-Whitney Psychiatric Clinic at the New York Hospital–Cornell Medical Center, not far from her apartment. She was told to come back on April 19 for tests. After taking the tests, she was asked to return on April 27, when she learned therapy would cost $40 an hour. Impossible.

Now she did not know where to go. Somehow she got through May and June, stumbling to work in the morning, wandering home at noon to fall on the bed, going nowhere at night, seeing no one outside the office.

Loren called to tell her Dr. Hartogs refused to take part in a deposition, a pretrial examination in the presence of a notary public. Bob brought a motion before the court to compel Dr. Hartogs to appear for a deposition, and Dr. Hartogs arrived at Bob's office on June 30, 1971, accompanied by his attorney, Jesse Cohen, a man in his fifties with white hair and a husky voice.

It was a waste of time. Except for stating his name, Dr. Hartogs would not answer a single question. Jesse Cohen answered each query for him by replying, "The witness refuses to answer on the ground that it may tend to incriminate him." Dr. Hartogs would not even answer Bob's questions about his educational background.

After Loren told her about the failed deposition, she asked him, "Didn't you think his eyes were piercing?"

"We couldn't see his eyes," said Loren. "He wore dark glasses."

Cohen was asking, "While you were under treatment by Dr. Hartogs, did you have sex with any other men?"

"Yes, I did," she said.

"And can you recall how many experiences you had, with how many different men?"

"Approximately four or five."

"And they all occurred during the period of treatment with Dr. Hartogs?"

"No. Two before, and two after." She had misunderstood his original question.

Judge Myers asked, "Heterosexual relationships prior to commencing your treatment with Dr. Hartogs?"

"Not relationships," she said.

"Sexual intercourse?" asked the judge.

"Yes," she said.

Cohen asked, "Did you discuss with Dr. Hartogs those heterosexual experiences?"

"No. . . ."

Once in a while, maybe every six months, she would feel the urge to have a glass of wine at dinner, then go out and pick up a strange man and spend the night with him at a hotel or motel. She wanted to be with men who didn't ask a lot of questions, who, like herself, were interested in being with someone just for the night, then separating.

She did not go to the singles bars uptown, but to a jazz bar on the Lower East Side called Slug's. There the men didn't care where you came from, or who your parents were. There was always a band made up of musicians who wandered in because they wanted to play together. Hers was usually the only white face there.

One night after a cocktail party and dinner at the Four Seasons given by the advertising department of *Esquire* for visiting advertisers, she found herself riding downtown in a cab with one of the guests, who said he would like to accompany her to Slug's. They walked east from Fifth Avenue and, as they plunged deeper into the East Village, her escort said, "I don't like this neighborhood. It's too seamy."

Julie was not uncomfortable because she had lived there, and Anne still did.

When they reached Avenue A, the man said, "I don't think we should go any farther."

"Do what you want," she said. "I'm going to Slug's."

He left her and she walked on alone.

She sat at the bar, sipping a glass of wine. She listened to the beat of the jazz, smiled at the musicians. The drummer was young, black, handsome, friendly. When Slug's closed, he asked if she would like to leave with him.

They caught a cab on Third Street, he gave an address, and they sped north. When the cab stopped, he discovered he had no money. She had none either. The driver, furious, drove them to the nearest police station. As the musician stepped out of the car, he handed her his drumsticks, saying, "Watch these for me, love, I'll be right back." He and the cab driver vanished into the night.

She waited for what seemed an hour, then left the taxi, hoping the drumsticks would be safe on the rear seat. In a bar she asked a young man if he would give her a dime to make a phone call, and he did. She called Chris, with whom she was living at the time.

"I'm stranded uptown and have no money to get home," she said. "Will you pay the fare if I find a cab?"

"Of course," said Chris.

She managed to locate a cab and the driver waited outside the Charles Street apartment while she ran upstairs and got the money. She had been lucky, she realized, to get out of such a jam so easily.

Another night she met a very attractive young blond man, who turned out to be a poet, when she was walking along Park Avenue in the Seventies. She was living by herself then, and she took him home for the night. In the morning he did not want to leave. He was lonely, just as she was, but she did not want to see him again. She did not wish any emotional entanglement.

Fortunately, in her few sexual forays, she did not meet a Jack the Ripper; neither the poet nor the drummer treated her with anything but respect. She had a dim awareness that her escapades, seldom though they occurred, showed how little she cared what she did with her life.

She never drank alone, no matter how depressed she felt. Nor did she have to drink to find men sexually attractive. But she found it hard to talk to a man after sleeping with him, to be around a man for hours at a time. She was frightened of men, socially and intellectually, she supposed because she had never been around a man in her early life.

She did not have this kind of difficulty getting along with a woman—but then, most of her early life had been spent alone with her mother, so it made sense. She did not think of herself as a lesbian, though after her affair with Chris she knew she liked women—a lot. But she liked men too. Usually she felt turned on by someone who was turned on by her.

Cohen was asking, "Julie, when, after May, 1971, did you see a psychiatrist or psychologist or any professional, in connection with your emotional disorder?"

"July of 1971, about two months after I terminated with Dr. Anderson. . . ."

It was July again, the horror month. She was crying more than ever, staying home from work, thinking obsessively of killing Dr. Hartogs, then herself. She took pills to keep going.

On the evening of July 8, she discovered she was out of the Dexamyl spansules Dr. Hartogs had given her. She desperately needed the lift a Dex always gave, so she decided to walk to Payne-Whitney and ask for a new prescription.

When she entered the emergency room, it must have been about eleven. A nurse asked, "What's wrong?"

She tried to speak but no words came out. She could only cry.

"What's your name?" asked the nurse.

She wrote it on a dusty desk by tracing the letters with her finger. The nurse asked if she had ever been a patient at Payne-Whitney and she nodded her head, remembering the tests.

Then she stood up, intending to leave, but they would not let her. All night she sat in the emergency room, crying, mute. She thought, When you're so angry that you are afraid you may destroy yourself and everyone around you, you can only sit in terror, immobilize your arms, your legs, your tongue, so you won't betray your rage. There were no words to describe her fury at being exploited sexually, her even greater fury at being abandoned. Dr. Hartogs had taken away what little identity she had, reducing her to a messy pulp.

To her, he had become father *and* mother. She had gone to him for help, as a terrified, hurt, and angry child who did not understand the torments inflicted on her. She wanted a better life, she wanted him to help her understand her feelings, she wanted to forgive her emotionally disturbed parents, who just did not know how to raise healthy children—one killed himself and now she was groping her way through the maze of daily living wearing blinders.

Instead of helping her he had used her—and then deserted her.

And because she thought of him as the substitute for her mother and father, the sexual relationship was like an incestuous affair. No matter what her participation, he had taken the Hippocratic oath, which said a doctor should not become sexually involved with a patient. Ever. Committed to healing, he had destroyed. It was as though a surgeon deliberately cut off a leg that could have been saved by a salve.

How could she say all this to a stranger? She was too enraged even to think clearly. All she knew was that she had been betrayed.

In the morning a nurse told her, "We called a cab."

Some orderlies helped her out to the street and she saw the "cab" was an ambulance. She fought as fiercely as she could but they forced her into it. She thought she would be taken to Bellevue, but the ambulance stopped in front of Metropolitan Hospital at 1901 First Avenue.

In the admitting room, a nurse started writing down the information sent from Payne-Whitney. At that moment Anne showed up—the nurse at Payne-Whitney had called her—rushed over to Julie, and kissed her.

She no longer felt so upset, but she still could not talk, even to Anne. A nurse brought the traditional white garb, asked her to take off her clothes and put it on. Anne said to the nurse, "Julie needs a more private place," and she was allowed to change in a closet.

But when they took her upstairs she became frightened, thinking, This is my first trip to a madhouse.

She was surprised to find herself in a ward that held both men and women. There were few whites, mostly blacks and Puerto Ricans. The ward consisted of seven large bedrooms, six patients to a room. Each room had a curtain instead of a door, and sometimes men would pull aside the curtain to her room and peek in at her.

As she lay on her bed, other patients came up and asked, "What are you in for?" as though it were a jail.

She could not answer, and as soon as they realized she was mute, they stopped asking. She was so weary from having been awake all night that she fell asleep at once.

Anne and Evan came to see her. Still she remained silent. Anne tried to cheer her up by drawing cartoons. One showed Julie hiding in a toilet bowl, only her eyes peering out over the rim. Anne also brought her cheese and peppers from a Middle East store.

Then Bob and Loren came. She communicated with them by writing notes.

Loren asked, "Why won't you talk to us?"

She wrote, "It's not that I won't talk. I *can't* talk."

She wrote a note to Bob: "Please get me out of here right away."

He said to her, "They won't let you leave before you can speak."

When she had been there a week the doctors gave her what she believed was Thorazine, the chemical straitjacket. Though she objected, she couldn't fake swallowing it because it was in liquid form. A few hours later she felt dazed, moved at the pace of a sleepwalker, eyes glassy.

The next morning she woke with a deadly headache. Needing to urinate, she stood up and lurched toward the bathroom. She blacked out. When she came to, she was lying on the floor near the wash basin.

A nurse was tugging at her, saying, "Get up! Get up!"

She could not move. She felt searing pains in her right hand and her head.

The nurse called another nurse and together they tried to lift her. One of the nurses accidentally stood on her long hair as they tried to pull her up, and she couldn't even scream at the pain.

Somehow they raised her, put her in a wheelchair, took her back to her bed, and called a doctor. There was a huge throbbing lump on her head. She thought she must have hit it on the basin as she fell to the floor.

There was also something wrong with her right thumb. It was turning purple and swelling up, as well as hurting. She wondered how this would affect her piano playing. She also had welts and bruises on the backs of both legs.

She saw her face in a mirror and realized what the phrase meant, "a face as white as a sheet." She felt nauseous all day.

A nurse took her for X rays, and they walked what seemed blocks. As they waited for an elevator she collapsed on the floor. The nurse told her to stand up. Painfully, she stumbled to her feet.

According to the X rays nothing had been broken, though she thought her thumb might well be.

One afternoon, a doctor whom she liked because he seemed interested in her asked, "How are you feeling?"

"I'm feeling better," she said.

These were the first words she had spoken in eight days.

Dr. Paul Schneck, the chief psychiatrist on the ward, visited her. He too seemed concerned about her. He was a slight man with brown hair, he had a pleasant face, and she liked the way he spoke, choosing words thoughtfully. She told him she was anxious to leave the hospital now that she could again speak.

She wrote Bob a letter:

First, I want to thank both you and Loren for coming. Was not too happy to be seen looking like such a zombie but I was enormously cheered by your visit.

Would suppose the surroundings appeared pretty grim to you, but I have no complaints. The staff are kind and for the most part do not hassle me. Was a little afraid of the other patients at first but ended up liking quite a few of them. The more violent ones were kept subdued with drugs. Fortunately I've no basis for comparison, but as madhouses go it didn't seem too bad. Except for the feeling of being locked up.

. . . Have had about three sessions with a Dr. Schneck, who is Chief Psychiatrist here. Did not want to talk to him, he being a shrink, but realized I was in no position to quibble. Explained it was all over between me and any psychiatrist. He suggested drug therapy, which I'm going to try. No talk, just medication. Am going to see him for this. Privately, not through the hospital. I'll be fine if I can think of him as my pusher rather than my psychiatrist.

Anyway, the reason for this rambling is he wants to talk to you. Told him I would ask you to call him. No objection to his talking to you. He assured me it was not his intention to dissuade you from going ahead with the case.

After eleven days in the hospital she was discharged. Several days later the hospital called to ask her to return, explaining, "The X rays show your thumb is broken. There was a mistake."

But she was on the outside and intended to stay there. She went instead to her own doctor, who sent her to a bone specialist, and he set the thumb. It remained plumper and shorter than the thumb of her left hand.

According to her hospital records, which she later saw, the night resident doctor who admitted her wrote:

Patient is mute and will not give information.

Personality Description: Patient described as aloof; lives alone and is depressed most of the time. She has compulsive eating episodes where she will devour all food in sight and then proceed to go on strict diet. At times patient will dress very neat and then have episodes of wearing unbecoming clothing. No history of religious affiliation though she comes from a strict Catholic family. History of suicidal thoughts, no attempts.

Mental Status: Patient appears mildly overweight, mute, sluggish but responsive to verbal comments. Sits with hands on wrist in clutching manner. Appears depressed and on verge of crying. Unable to further evaluate mental status due to patient's refusal to answer questions.

The diagnosis was: "psychotic depressive reaction, schizoid personality, catatonic schizophrenia, hysterical personality and transient situational disturbance."

She thought that about covered everything in the book.

She liked Dr. Schneck, and found she talked more freely to him than she had to Dr. Anderson or Dr. Hartogs. She told him of her sexual involvement with Dr. Hartogs and he listened sympathetically. He did not comment on the lawsuit except to say he hoped it would not hurt her further. She arranged to see him, starting in September, twice a week at his private office on Lexington Avenue and Eighty-seventh Street. For the first time she thought she might get help from a psychiatrist.

Though she had been absent from her job most of July, she still had eight weeks' vacation coming to her. She had taken no time off in seven years—where was there to go, and with whom? Now she felt she needed a vacation, and asked Evan if she could take two weeks. She had heard of a clinic in San Antonio, Texas, where people went on fasts as a way of relieving tension. She had lost fifteen pounds at the hospital, so for once she was not concerned about her body, but she thought fasting might help her mind.

She flew to San Antonio. She immediately liked the clinic, its concern with each guest, the fact it had no TV or radio. Her goal was to fast twelve days.

The first day she felt elated. The second day she was plain starved. She decided to tell the woman doctor who checked her physical condition every day that she was giving up the fast and wanted something—anything—to eat.

Then the man across the hall came into her room and told her he had fasted fifty-two days, and she felt embarrassed to be giving up after only one. Sensing her problem, he said, "Try to get through the second day. After that you'll be all right." Somehow she managed, and by the third day all hunger pains were gone. She felt serene, ethereal, almost high.

But by the tenth day she was so weak she could hardly draw a comb through her hair. She did not want to lose so much strength she couldn't take care of herself, so she called it quits. She was given carrot juice the first day, oranges the second. On the third day for lunch she was served lettuce, and she enjoyed it as much as if she had been a rabbit. For dinner she received cabbage leaves, celery stalks, and whole tomatoes, no dressing. The third day she was also allowed nuts, though no peanuts.

When she left after two weeks, she felt in a cooled-out state. She thought of the visit as an enforced vacation from thinking.

Then it was back to New York and her job, and the start of therapy with Dr. Schneck. In his office, as with Dr. Anderson, she did little but cry.

Cohen was asking, "Over what period of time were you seen by Dr. Schneck?"

"For about eight months starting in July, once a week at times, twice a week at other times."

"Was that continuously during this eight-month period?"

"Yes. . . ."

She was particularly grateful to be seeing Dr. Schneck because on October 8 she faced her first crisis in the lawsuit. She was to be the target of a deposition, a pretrial examination, conducted by Dr. Hartogs' lawyer, Jesse Cohen.

"I can't do it," she told Bob. "I'll say the wrong thing."

"Just tell the truth," he said. "The way it was."

She faced Jesse Cohen in his office at 295 Madison Avenue, and he asked her to describe her experiences from the day she first walked into Dr. Hartogs' office to the last time she saw him. Nervously, she did her best. Then he said, "Now, from the time you entered [the apartment] until the time you left, do you recall anything that occurred other than the fact that you made love?"

"No," she said, wondering what he meant.

"At the time you made love were you nude?"

"Yes," she said.

"Was the doctor nude?"

"Yes."

"In what room did you make love in his apartment?"

"The bedroom."

"Were the lights on or off?"

"I don't remember."

"On any occasion that you made love to Dr. Hartogs, was he nude other than this occasion?"

"Yes," she said, still wondering what Jesse Cohen was driving at.

"Can you tell us whether there was any gross physical mark or abnormality on Dr. Hartog's body?"

"No," she said. His body had appeared perfectly normal to her.

Jesse Cohen seemed puzzled. "You saw him in the nude on many occasions?" he asked.

"Yes," she said.

"On the occasion, on or about September eight, 1970, when you had intercourse with Dr. Hartogs in the bedroom of his apartment, will you describe just what he did and just what you did?"

"We made love," she said. "I don't think that needs any description."

Jesse Cohen asked if Dr. Hartogs told her he was seeing any other women.

"I don't think he said exactly that, he just implied it," she answered.

"Did he tell you he loved you?"

"Yes."

"Did he tell you that in order to induce you to have sexual relations with him?"

"I suppose it was an inducement, yes," she said.

"Can you tell us how frequently he told you he loved you?"

"No," she said.

"Were these on rare occasions or numerous occasions?"

"I think on rare occasions," she said. Actually, she could remember his saying it only once and writing it once, the time he signed the note, "Your affectionate rabbit."

Jesse Cohen also questioned her about her lesbian

relationship with Chris. He asked, "Did you tell Dr. Hartogs that you felt strongly attracted to women?"

"I didn't feel attractive to anybody," she said.

After the examination, Bob and Loren told her she did well. They used words like "lucid," "forthright," and "candid." Bob said, "The deposition was a preview and the reviews were raves." They asked her to take a psychological test, which she did, and was happy to learn her I.Q. was well above average.

She thought of Dr. Hartogs as obsessively as before. She worried, too, that her attorneys might not be compensated for all the time they were spending on her suit. Bob told her not to worry. Although the firm's usual policy was to bill on an hourly basis, Bob felt so strongly about the case that he told her if they were successful, she could pay them what she owed out of damages. She took her small savings and gave it to Bob to help defray the firm's out-of-pocket expenses.

Then once again she fell into depression, her way of holding back rage. She could barely drag herself to work in the mornings. She would leave at noon, go home and sleep for an hour or two, then, if she was able, crawl back and work until five. She cried uncontrollably as she walked along the street, in the subway, on the bus, in Dr. Schneck's waiting room as well as in his office. She had a sinus condition from the tears that were constantly irritating her eyes and nose. She used enormous amounts of Kleenex.

Then she stopped going to work, stopped seeing anyone at all. She had difficulty moving her limbs. She walked in slow motion; it took her twenty minutes to go twenty feet. She had to think, Now take one step, then the next, then another. She was sleeping twenty-one hours a day, getting up only for a daily shower and eating crackers to stay alive. Each time she woke, she would sit on the edge of the bed and think, Now I have to stand, walk across the floor, go into the bathroom, turn on the water.

It was as though the part that made her go was no longer inside her, as if her spirit had fled her body and was living outside her, spinning like a satellite.

She was convinced that only by killing Dr. Hartogs could she feel free. She did not tell this to Dr. Schneck, but she did tell him she planned to get a gun and kill herself.

When she went to his office for her next appointment, Dr. Schneck said to her, "I'd like you to go back to Metropolitan Hospital for a while."

"I don't want to," she said.

"What about a private hospital?" he asked. "It will be more expensive. Does your health insurance cover psychiatric care?"

It did not. Dr. Schneck repeated, "I feel very strongly that you should go to Metropolitan."

"I'm much better," she said. "I'm not crying any more."

Nor was she. The depression seemed to have lifted. Instead, she was as if in a stupor, feeling nothing.

Dr. Schneck suggested, "Why don't you meet me in the lobby at Metropolitan tomorrow at three o'clock and we'll talk it over?"

"O.K.," she said.

But she thought he might commit her, so she did not show up.

The next day, December 6, 1971, she went to his office for her regular appointment. He said, "I'm going to take you home to get your clothes and we're going to Metropolitan."

She had no energy to resist. He locked his office, got his car, drove to her apartment. He went upstairs with her, where she packed her overnight case, taking only a toothbrush and a pink woolen blanket. She did not like the drab, thin blankets the hospital provided.

Dr. Schneck drove her to Metropolitan Hospital, took care of her admission, and promised to visit her every day except weekends. She found herself on the same floor where she had been six months before, and in a similar ward. Three of the women in her room were senile, and she felt especially sorry for them.

She noticed that a young, slightly built man—a Tibetan, she learned—was always following one or another of the women around. He didn't speak a word of English. The second night, the lights had just been put out and she was almost asleep when a flashlight shone in her face. She saw the young Tibetan standing by her bed, his hand stretched out to her. Orderlies immediately took him away. Dr. Schneck later told her the young man would have done nothing to harm her.

Day after day she lay in her bed, sleeping, not caring who came or went. A young woman was admitted to the ward; she seemed brash, hostile, as though she owned the whole floor. Julie had a corner bed near a window, and one night, after lights were out, the newcomer rose from her bed and walked over to Julie. She stared at Julie, said not a word. Julie was uncomfortable but thought, In a mental hospital you have to make allowances for people. Then the woman moved closer to Julie.

Julie said, "Look, you've got your problems and I've got mine. Just leave me alone."

At that the woman picked up Julie's overnight case, which lay on the floor by her bed, and cavalierly carted it to the other side of the room. Then she walked back to Julie, empty-handed.

"Go get my night case," said Julie. She was frightened but she was angry, too.

The woman didn't move.

"You go get it," Julie commanded.

The woman merely went on staring.

Julie let out a howl, rose from her bed, and ran into the hall. She found a nurse and told her what had happened. The nurse retrieved Julie's overnight case and warned the newcomer to stay in her own bed. After that, the strange young woman never came near Julie but made faces at her from across the room.

"How do you expect me to improve when I'm constantly exposed to these upsetting experiences?" she asked Dr. Schneck. "This is no place to get better."

One resident proposed electroshock treatment and she said, "Under no circumstances. You can overpower me and force me to take it but I'll get you afterward. I may seem defenseless while I'm here but I've got lawyers to protect me." She heard no more about electroshock.

The visits by Dr. Schneck were the high point of each day. To think a psychiatrist would see her five days a week made her feel important. She felt she might eventually trust him.

She became less depressed, started to accept life around her, talked more freely to the nurses and other patients. She was discharged after five weeks, on January 6, 1972. It was the start of a new year.

She returned to her job and twice-a-week therapy with Dr. Schneck. She had lost the feeling of separation of body and spirit, and hoped it would never return. Though she still felt depressed, she thought she might pull herself out, with Dr. Schneck's help.

Seven days after her discharge from the hospital, she appeared for the continuation of her deposition at Jesse Cohen's office. Loren was present. At Jesse Cohen's request, she produced the canceled checks she had given Dr. Hartogs, seventy-one in all, as well as twenty-two canceled checks made out to Dr. Anderson and nine to Dr. Schneck. Jesse Cohen questioned her at length about her visits to psychiatrists and her two hospitalizations.

The last session of the deposition took place on May 22. Jesse Cohen asked about the drugs she had taken in Dr. Hartogs' office, trying to find out if in any way they had affected her consciousness. She said her mind was "often not clear," though she was always "aware" when she had sexual intercourse.

Jesse Cohen asked if Dr. Hartogs had ever used force. She mentioned the one time she had not felt like sex, had told him so, but that did not stop him.

"What did he do? Did he pull your legs apart?" asked Jesse Cohen.

"Yes," she said.

"Forcefully?"

"I don't think it took too much force because I get very limp."

"On this occasion when you became limp, had you taken any drugs in his presence?"

"I don't remember."

Jesse Cohen asked if she knew, each time she went to Dr. Hartogs' office, that she was going to have sexual intercourse.

"It was quite likely that we would," she said. Yet she felt she never could take anything for granted with Dr. Hartogs.

Cohen was saying, "Julie, after your release from your second admission to Metropolitan Hospital, did you continue seeing Dr. Schneck?"

"Yes, I did. Until early summer of 1972," she said.

"Did you continue working for *Esquire* magazine during this period of time?"

"Yes. I went in every day, and sometimes I would stay all day, sometimes I wouldn't. I didn't think my work was as good as it should be. I was depressed."

"Did there come a time when you left your employment with *Esquire* magazine?"

"I left there in May, 1973."

"Why did you decide to leave?"

"I had no more interest in doing the work there. I had no plans. I just didn't want to work there anymore."

Her life was moving quickly now; she made several important decisions. She wanted to leave *Esquire,* and she was tired of New York. She decided to fly to San Francisco, this time to stay. She notified Bob and Loren where she would be, promising to fly east the minute they needed her.

She no longer feared Dr. Hartogs, and no longer felt

she needed a gun. She had two young attorneys who would wage her fight for her—within the law.

Cohen was asking, "Do you remember what you were earning when you left *Esquire?*"

"I was earning about two hundred dollars a week."

"When you went to San Francisco, did you become employed?"

"Not for about six or eight months."

"Can you tell us, please, what job you undertook?"

"Selling in a store. A clerk."

"What were you being paid?"

"About sixty-five dollars a week."

"And have you been in therapy in San Francisco?"

"Yes, I have. I see a therapist at Laguna Honda Hospital one hour a week, and I have group therapy two hours a week."

At that point Judge Myers called a recess until the following morning at ten.

Her first day as a witness was over, and she felt deep relief. As Bob, Loren, and she rode back to the office, they again praised her testimony. They remarked that not a smile, not a frown had passed over the face of any member of the jury while she was on the witness stand.

Bob told her that an even tougher chore lay in store the next day, when she would be cross-examined by Mr. Halpern. Although Jesse Cohen was still chief counsel for Dr. Hartogs, he was not expected to appear because he was ill. Mr. Halpern, at seventy-two, had years of trial experience behind him.

To prepare her, Bob asked her to stay at the office that evening so that Asher Lans, the senior member of the firm, could conduct a mock cross-examination. He knew the case well, having listened to Bob and Loren discuss it, and he was a total stranger to her, as Mr. Halpern would be.

"We don't think anybody could cross-examine you better than Asher," Bob told her.

Mr. Lans was courteous, and she liked him, but she found his questions disturbing. He probed deeply into the sexual episodes, accusing her of lying. When he demanded to know whether she had brought the suit simply to get even with Dr. Hartogs, she burst into tears.

Loren sat silent, listening. Later he said to her, "It hurt me to see you hurt, but it would have been a disservice to try to make it easier. You had to get a flavor of what's to come." She knew he was right.

She expected to have a hard time with Mr. Halpern. When the trial first opened, four days before, he had nearly succeeded in having her case dismissed.

She recalled how at ten o'clock sharp, the judge's law secretary had appeared at a door to the left of the judge's bench and motioned the court officer to approach. This meant Judge Myers was ready to start. The officer rose, walked to the door, and rapped on it three times to attract the attention of the spectators.

Judge Myers, decorous in his black judicial gown, walked in. His dark hair was flecked with gray, his mustache well groomed. He had been on the bench nine years and was known as a fair and impartial judge. The publication *Town & Village,* which reported on the Kips Bay area of New York, where he lived with his wife, Roslyn, a teacher of handicapped children, once said in an editorial, "Myers is a man with a conscience and the courage to match it."

Judge Myers had protected the civil rights of the accused in criminal cases dealing with illegal wire tapping, illegal search and seizure, and the right to a speedy trial. He had protected consumers, motorists (from damages inflicted by the negligence of New York City in towaway operations), and tenants (from slum landlords). He had a continuing interest in the rehabilitation of prisoners he sentenced. In 1954, before he became a judge, he had sparked a campaign for improved educational facilities in New York by refusing to send his daughter to the old P.S. 19 in the Stuyvesant Town area. He contended the school was unfit and, by suit, compelled the city to shut down the old school and build a new one.

In an autobiographical sketch, Judge Myers once wrote:

I was born on December 12, 1912, at 197 Madison Street, an unheated tenement house in a slum neighborhood on the lower east side of Manhattan. My father was a laborer's helper. I lived with him, my mother and two younger brothers in a small apartment on the third floor of this tenement. There was no heat except for a coal stove in the kitchen; no electricity except gas light for many years; no bathroom or bath; the toilet, shared with a neighboring family, was in the public hall. I lived in this apartment until I was married in 1936. I attended college and law school at night while working during the day in factories and at other menial jobs in order to earn my tuition and contribute to the support of my family. Since my marriage, I have lived in the same community where I have been continuously involved in community affairs.

The court officer announced, "All rise. Trial Term, Part Twenty-one, is now in session, Honorable Allen Murray Myers presiding." Everyone stood. Judge Myers mounted the bench and said, "Please be seated." There was no gavel, just quiet procedure. Then the judge turned to the court officer and said, "Mr. Sherlock, please bring in the jury."

Julie had been surprised to learn there were only six jurors (plus an alternate) in Civil Court, and their decision did not have to be unanimous, but by a five-member majority.

Bob, Loren, and she had spent hours discussing the type of juror they would prefer. They felt that ethnic background was irrelevant, but wanted a middle-class jury. They hoped mainly for women, in the belief that they went to doctors in greater numbers than men, and would understand the trust a patient places in a physician. If there were men, they wanted married men who might worry about their wives' being subjected to sexual advances by a doctor. In essence they wanted a jury that would understand how an emotionally troubled young woman seeking help could have the misfortune to find a doctor who took advantage of her sexually, thus causing her to become even more emotionally troubled.

It took the better part of a day for attorneys representing both sides to select the jury. Each lawyer was allowed three challenges "without cause" and as many as he wished "for cause." Mr. Halpern rejected several white, single career women, who might be expected to be sympathetic to Julie. Bob excused a young white man attending law school because his brother was a lawyer Bob had known professionally.

About half the candidates considered were white, half black. By sheer chance—"incredible chance," Bob said —all the jurors finally selected were black. There were four women and two men. All were between the ages of thirty-five and forty-five; all were hard-working family people who had held their jobs a long time. Two worked in hospitals, one as an administrator, the other as a cook. One juror was a warehouseman, one a supervisor for the telephone company, one a supervisor for the welfare department, and one a teacher of mentally retarded children.

Julie watched now as the jurors filed in. The "foreman" was a woman, and she sat in the chair nearest the judge.

It was the plaintiff's right to be heard first, so Bob asked, "Your Honor, may I proceed?"

"Yes, you may proceed," said the judge.

Each side made an opening statement. Then Bob said, "I call the plaintiff, Julie Roy."

But before she could even stand up, Mr. Halpern rose to say, "Your Honor, please, I reserve my motion on the opening."

The judge said, "You can do anything you want."

"Well, I wouldn't want to make it in the presence of the jury," said Mr. Halpern.

"You want the jury to leave?" the judge asked.

"Yes," said Mr. Halpern.

"Gentlemen of the jury, step out of the box," said the judge.

She wondered what the four women jurors thought, addressed as "gentlemen." She also wondered what was coming; she had never heard of a trial starting this way.

After the jury left, Mr. Halpern asked that the case be dismissed. He claimed the suit was barred by Section 80A of the New York State Civil Rights Act. This section abolished civil damage actions sought on a variety of grounds, including seduction.

He cited a case that had been dismissed in 1971 by Supreme Court Justice James Leff in a decision barring seduction as grounds for a malpractice action against a doctor. Mr. Halpern said that case, in which a doctor had intercourse with a female patient he was treating for physical ailments, was similar to the one presently before the court.

Bob asked to look at the case, which had been published in the *New York Law Journal*. After reading it, he told the judge the two cases were not similar. Dr. Hartogs was a psychiatrist, not a gynecologist, as in Judge Leff's case, and the other patient did not go to her doctor for treatment of mental illness. Bob pointed out that the American Psychiatric Association, to which most of the psychiatrists of the nation belong, had stated in 1972 that for a psychiatrist to have sex with a patient was unethical, and therefore it was "fraudulent misrepresentation" for a psychiatrist to claim that having sex with a patient was therapy.

Bob concluded, "I can't believe psychiatrists are given *carte blanche* to sleep with their patients. That is not what Section Eighty-A was intended for."

The judge said that if there were proof that Julie had

been made physically or mentally helpless by some drug or other physical means, and if the jury were able to find from the evidence that she had sex with the psychiatrist not by persuasion but by some other "force" that deprived her of "informed consent," then Section 80A would not apply.

Bob explained to Judge Myers that the psychological process known as "transference," which is presumed to take place in every case of psychological therapy, accomplished the same thing as a drug. The judge commented, "I can see now that this statute, according to *your* interpretation, would be applicable to every professional except a psychiatrist."

The judge then asked the jurors to return. He told them he was in the middle of acting on a motion made by one of the attorneys involving a question of law, and that he wanted to give the lawyers an opportunity to do more research and continue their arguments, so he was announcing a recess until the following morning at ten.

In her heart Julie wanted the trial to go on, but a part of her was relieved at the thought she might not have to testify—though she would never dare admit this to her attorneys.

That afternoon Bob, Loren, and Julie shared a taxi uptown to the firm's office. Bob and Loren appeared concerned by Mr. Halpern's motion to dismiss the case. Before the trial even got off the ground they might have to go to a higher court for an appeal.

This was her first legal emergency. At the office that afternoon and evening, she sat in on a brainstorming session with Bob, Loren, and three other lawyers who were to help out substantially during the trial: Deborah Lans, Malcolm I. Lewin, known as Nick, and Sol V.

Slotnik. These three formed what Miss Lans called the "crisis research team," standing ready through the duration of the trial to find answers to any legal question that might arise. They established communication with Bob and Loren during the day through public telephones in the corridor just outside the courtroom. Usually other lawyers picked up the phone when it rang and sent messages to Bob or Loren that he had a call.

That evening Loren, Nick Lewin, and Sol Slotnik went to the library of the Association of the Bar of the City of New York to read what few decisions there were on psychiatric malpractice, as well as law-review articles and other commentaries. They traced the historical antecedents of the seduction statutes in this country, England, and other nations. They reached the conclusion that Mr. Halpern's motion must be denied: There was a definite distinction between doctors' using sex as psychotherapy and doctors' indulging in sex with patients without any claim that it was a form of treatment.

When court reconvened the next day Bob told the judge there had been no time to write a brief, but that an oral argument would be made by his partner, Loren Plotkin.

Loren argued that, in Julie's case, seduction was not the issue, as in the case described by Judge Leff. The issue was "a simple, standard, common-law malpractice case in which the nature of the malpractice, instead of being a sponge left inside a patient, is the fact that sexual relations were prescribed and had a tremendously deleterious effect," he explained.

He discussed the nature of transference, which, he explained, occurred when the patient related to the therapist as he had done when a child to his mother and father, trusting the therapist implicitly as to all decisions.

"Transference," he said, "deprives a patient of the ability to use his own judgment."

He described it as a concept originating in the work of Dr. Sigmund Freud, calling it a medical phenomenon that had certain effects on a patient. He said, "Precisely because it has these effects on a patient, a sexual relationship between a psychiatrist and a patient is forbidden from the time of Freud to the present time." He repeated with emphasis, "It is forbidden."

Though Julie was seated, her knees had felt weak as Loren presented his argument. The judge seemed to her gruff and unsympathetic, and he didn't hesitate to interrupt with questions. Mr. Halpern added to the confusion by constantly objecting. She soon would have been confused and crying, but Loren stayed cool and polite, and never faltered. He answered all the judge's questions, then continued with his argument. It seemed to her that all his ideas were arranged in intangible little boxes that he moved around inside his head, never losing track of any of them.

The judge gave Bob and Loren additional time to submit a formal brief. He said he would reserve his decision, then adjourned the trial until Monday morning.

The taxi ride uptown was a bit more cheerful than the previous day's. That afternoon Julie sat in the office with Bob and Loren as they and the crisis research team worked on the brief. Later Bob went to a dinner party at his home, arranged before the date of the trial had been set. His guests told him, "You can't possibly win—how is anyone going to believe the word of this

sick girl against that of a well-known psychiatrist?"
Lawyers outside the firm said substantially the same
thing. Yet to Bob and Loren it seemed obvious they *had*
to win because they were in the right, and what Dr.
Hartogs had done seemed so wrong.

Julie was depressed by this latest unexpected hurdle
placed in their way by Mr. Halpern. In the previous
four years, Dr. Hartogs' lawyers had taken an appeal
at virtually every juncture, creating repeated delays.

Bob and Loren had spent thousands of hours on the
case. Several times judges suggested the claim be settled
out of court, but Bob steadfastly refused. Julie had told
him she wanted Dr. Hartogs brought to trial. Bob understood that to her the case was primarily about her right
to tell the truth, secondarily about money. He told
Loren, "I think of this case not in terms of litigation but
in terms of Julie." He told her, "I'm glad I don't get
this emotionally involved in every case."

Bob and Loren worked so well together, she enjoyed
seeing them in action. Loren told her, "Everyone thinks
we're just a couple of young lawyers who will eventually
give up, but they don't know us." At the time they
brought suit Loren was twenty-seven, Bob thirty-one.

They made her part of every conference, kept her
informed of what they were doing. They listened to and
sometimes incorporated her suggestions as they planned
trial strategy. They were the only men she had ever
known who fought for her, and at no point put her
down.

Bob felt it vital to get the brief to Judge Myers and
Mr. Halpern by Saturday afternoon. He did not want
Mr. Halpern receiving their thirty-five-page brief Mon-

day morning and saying he needed time to read it, thus causing further delay.

Since there was little heat in the office over weekends, Bob turned his apartment on Park Avenue into a second office. Everyone congregated there as Bob wrote the final draft of the brief. It was typed, and that afternoon hand-delivered to Judge Myers.

Mr. Halpern lived in Rockland County, about fifty miles northwest of New York City, and Bob arranged for a messenger to deliver a copy of the brief to his home. But when Bob phoned to tell Mr. Halpern of the arrangement, there was no answer. So he called Mr. Halpern's assistant, who lived in Queens, and the assistant picked up the copy that afternoon.

With the brief completed, several questions remained unanswered. Would the trial proceed on Monday, or would Judge Myers dismiss it on Mr. Halpern's motion? If it proceeded, would Dr. Hartogs show up, after pleading the Fifth Amendment for four years? If he did not appear, the jury might consider his absence a confession of guilt.

If he did appear to testify, what would his defense be? Bob and Loren thought Mr. Halpern would argue one of three ways: either that she was lying outright; or that she was delusional, a "schizophrenic, of the catatonic, withdrawn type," who would get "progressively worse"—this was what Dr. Walter Brinitzer, the psychiatrist slated to testify in behalf of Dr. Hartogs, had said of her after an hour's interview in 1973; or that he had had sex with her because it was his professional opinion that it would be beneficial to her condition.

Nick Lewin said he believed Dr. Hartogs would appear and testify but would hold off advising both the court and the plaintiff's attorneys of his defense until as late as possible. By waiting until the plaintiff's evidence was in, he would be in a position to shape his defense in accordance with Julie's testimony. Nick also said a number of lawyers in the courthouse who were following the case predicted Dr. Hartogs would claim he never had intercourse with her and try to show some physical impediment that prevented him from having sex.

On Monday morning, Judge Myers, after reading Bob's brief, ruled the trial was to proceed. Now she faced her second day of testimony.

6

Julie felt less nervous the second day. Again Dr. Hartogs did not appear; she did not have to worry about his eyes, his anger. Bob had not finished his direct examination, so she faced him first.

He asked, "Julie, could you tell us, please, whether you presently think about the therapy you had with Dr. Hartogs, and whether you have thought about it since you moved to San Francisco?"

"Yes, I continue to think about it very often. . . ."

She thought of her two years in San Francisco as a kind of running away, but sometimes that was how you saved your life. She lived six months at an ashram, a Hindu religious retreat, then got a job as a clerk in a bookstore, working sixteen hours a week for $65. She answered an ad for a share-the-rent arrangement and moved to a modest house where she lived with a man and woman to whom she rarely spoke.

She led a lonely existence. Several men had asked her for dates, others tried to approach her on the street, but she refused them all. Going to group therapy once a week for two hours was the most social thing she did. For a year she had sat in the group paralyzed with fear, but now she was talking more, taking baby steps to emotional health. At the insistence of Carmen Lynch, one of the group leaders, she also had individual sessions with a woman therapist.

She thought of herself as going through a period of catching her breath. She had a few women friends but no one to take the place of Anne; they had drifted apart, and she had not even called Anne on her return to New York. She liked the woman psychologist who led the group but didn't trust the man, a hangover from her experience with Dr. Hartogs. She had been afraid to tell her new therapists what had happened to her; they might be reluctant to treat a patient who had had a sexual relationship with a psychiatrist to whom she had gone for treatment. Some of the men in the group told her she was too closed off, though she did not feel that way.

She sensed that slowly she was acquiring more faith in herself, becoming more comfortable around strangers, not so frightened friends would forsake her once they knew her. She could now like someone without feeling she had a big investment in that person. Nor did she force herself to smile and be sweet all the time. She saw her former sweetness as a façade. Now she'd rather be a wet blanket than fake a feeling.

The pleasure of her life was still music. She had her piano shipped from New York, and found a piano teacher at the San Francisco Conservatory of Music. One day, while waiting for her lesson, she played her teacher's harpsichord and loved the soft sound. She sold her piano and rented a harpsichord, hoping eventually to build her own.

By the time Loren called her in November, 1974, to tell her a date had been set for the trial, she had saved $300, the exact cost of plane fare, but not a penny more.

She wondered how she would pay for a hotel and meals. Almost the minute she hung up on Loren's call, the doorbell rang. The mailman stood there with a special-delivery letter. It contained a check for $1,300 from her employee profit sharing at *Esquire*.

Before she left San Francisco, she thought carefully about what clothes to take and, in addition to the clothes she wore on the first day of the trial, packed a lavender turtleneck sweater and a second ankle-length skirt of dark red, which she had also made.

Loren reserved a room for her at the Allerton Hotel on East Fifty-seventh Street. He said his secretary had spent a day searching for a place that was comfortable, not expensive, and near the office so she could walk there each morning and share a taxi to the courthouse.

Cohen finished his direct examination and Halpern rose to take over the cross-examination. "Miss Roy," he began, "would you please speak up so I can hear you all the way down here and the last juror can hear you there?"

"Yes," she said.

He asked questions about her birthplace, her schooling, her work in Chicago, and her marriage. "During the period of a year and a half that you were married, did you have satisfactory sexual relations with your husband?"

"It was satisfactory in the beginning. It was not satisfactory at the end," she said.

"For how long a period was it satisfactory and for how long was it not satisfactory?"

"It was satisfactory for about a year, not satisfactory for about half a year."

"Would you tell this jury why?"

"Because I didn't love him anymore."

"Did you have a lesbian relationship during that period of time?"

"No," she said.

"When did you start having the lesbian relationships?" he asked.

"About 1963," she said. Having survived Mr. Lans's mock cross-examination, she knew Mr. Halpern would try to pry into the details of her sex life, and she was able to answer his questions calmly.

"Did you have any relationship with any man in 1965?" he asked.

"No, not that I remember," she said.

"Well, didn't you testify yesterday that before '68 you had sexual relationships with two men?"

"Yes," she said. "But I don't remember when. It was sometime prior to seeing Dr. Hartogs."

"Who were these men that you had sexual relationships with?"

"I don't know who they were," she said.

"Where did you meet man number one?"

She said she had met both men in a bar in the Village.

"Now, isn't it a fact that during this period, before you went to Dr. Hartogs, you engaged quite frequently in imbibing alcoholic drinks?"

"No, that's not so," she said.

"Well, did you drink quite often?"

"No," she said.

"About how frequently would you go out and get drunk?"

"Perhaps once every six months."

"And was it at that time that you went down to the Village to pick up some man?"

"No. I went down to hear the music they played at this bar."

"My question is, when you got drunk, did you go down to the Village to pick up any man to take him home and sleep with him?"

"No. No, sir," she said.

"Never have?"

"That wasn't the reason I went down to the Village."

The judge asked, "Where did you have sex with them?"

"One time it was in a hotel downtown and another time I went to his apartment," she said.

Halpern asked, "What hotel did you have this sex in?"

"I don't remember the hotel," she said.

"Did you stay all night with him?"

"Yes."

"Did you have more than one act of intercourse with him?"

"I don't remember."

"Now, you said you went to the other man's apartment. Where was that?"

"I don't remember."

"Did you stay all night with him there, too?"

"Yes," she said.

"How many acts of intercourse did you have that night?"

"I don't remember."

Halpern wanted to know whether Dr. Hartogs had asked if she had a sexual relationship with any man prior to 1968, except her husband, and she said he did ask and that she had told him no.

"Was that the truth or just a lie?"

"That was the truth."

"Didn't you just testify that you had sexual relations with two men you met in a bar?"

"I had sex with each man one time. I didn't have a relationship with either man," she said.

Halpern asked her weight at that time, and she said she did not remember. He wanted to know if she "devoured a pound of candy or a pint of ice cream in one session."

"Not the candy, no. The ice cream, yes," she said.

Halpern asked about the blue Marimekko dress that she said she had worn for two years, day in and day out. He asked if she stayed in bed for long spells and she said she did, adding, "My physical body didn't feel sick but I didn't feel well in my mind."

He questioned her about sex with Dr. Hartogs, asking if she had engaged in cunnilingus, and she said, "That's correct."

"How often?" he asked.

"I don't remember how often."

"And you also testified, did you not, that you engaged in fellate [sic]. I don't know if I am pronouncing it correctly."

"Yes," she said.

"How often?"

"I don't remember."

In response to further questioning, she said she had written Dr. Hartogs "love letters" during therapy. Halpern asked, "Did you fall in love with him?"

"Yes, I was in love with him," she said.

"Did he tell you that he loved you?"

"Yes, he did."

Questioning her about the frequency of intercourse, Halpern asked, "Were there days when you had sexual intercourse with him three times a day?"

"There was an occasion, yes," she replied.

"Were there occasions when you had it twice a day?"

"Yes."

"Was that in between treatment of patients?"

"No, it was during my treatment and then perhaps later in the afternoon."

"Did you look forward to them?"

"I don't remember."

"You weren't forced into that, were you?"

"I was not physically tied down, no."

"But you enjoyed the sex with him, didn't you?"

"Sometimes I did and sometimes I didn't."

Halpern asked, "Did there come a time when Dr. Hartogs said to you he didn't want to have any more dealings with you?"

"I don't remember if he said that," she said.

"Well, what did he say in words or substance?"

"He didn't want to see me anymore."

"That made you very angry, didn't it?"

"I don't remember if I was angry. I was extremely upset."

"Isn't it a fact that you called him and said you had broken your arm?"

"Yes, I did."

"That was a lie, wasn't it?"

"Yes, it was."

"And you didn't want to come back to him anymore, isn't that right?"

"That's right."

"You never went back to him, is that right?"

"That's correct."

"Now, did you feel jilted at that time?"

"I felt betrayed. I didn't feel jilted."

"Well, let me ask you about this betrayal. You, with a clear mind, knowing what you are doing, entered into this sexual relationship with him, did you not?"

"I entered into the sexual treatment with him."

"Did you enter this sexual relationship with him?"

"It was a sexual *treatment,*" she said.

Halpern said, "You are not a psychiatrist, are you?"

Judge Myers put in, "Come on. Let's not get into semantics."

"All right," said Halpern to the judge. Then to Julie, "Isn't it a fact that you were so irate that you intended in your mind killing him?"

"Yes, I thought about killing him," she said.

"Did you go out to look for a gun with the intention of killing him?"

"It was the following summer. The summer of 1971."

"After you left Dr. Hartogs, after the nineteen months that you were with him, did you have the same feeling of depression?"

"Only worse," she said.

"Did you have the same feeling of being unable to make friends or acquaintances?"

"Yes, I had that feeling."

"Did you have any feelings of hate against men?"

"I was afraid of men."

He asked again about the two men she had sexual intercourse with, wanted to know the name of the bar where she had met them.

"Slug's," she said.

He asked if she went to work the following morning, after spending the night with a man, and she said she did not remember. Then he asked, "Did you ever resume a lesbian relationship after you left Dr. Hartogs?"

"Yes," she said.

"When did you resume your lesbian relationship?"

"I believe it was in 1972."

"For how long a period of time?"

"We were together about a little over a year."

Halpern asked, "When did you leave Dr. Hartogs?"

"In September of 1970," she said.

Then Halpern said, "Miss Roy, you testified that both you and Dr. Hartogs were on his couch and both were nude, isn't that right?"

"Yes."

"How wide would you say that couch was? Just show us with your hands, if you can't figure."

She illustrated with her hands. Cohen said, "Approximately four feet."

The judge said, "Four feet. We all agree approximately four feet."

Halpern said to her, "Tell us this. While you and Dr. Hartogs were both in the nude on this couch, did you have the lights on or did you have the lights off?"

"The lights would be on most of the time."

"Can you tell us any mark on his body that was abnormal?"

"The only thing that I remember that was a little abnormal, he had a funny vein in one of his legs. I don't remember which leg."

"Aside from the funny vein in one of his legs, did you see anything else abnormal?"

"No."

"Didn't you tell this jury that you fondled his testicles and his penis?"

"Yes, I did."

"Did you see anything abnormal there?"

"No."

"Now, as far as his bodily condition is concerned, is there anything unusual about it?"

"He had a lot of hair."

Halpern asked questions about what Dr. Hartogs' apartment looked like, and then Judge Myers announced a recess for lunch.

The courtroom was left unlocked so they could work on the afternoon's questions. Bob and Loren congratulated her, saying they were surprised to find she sounded more "fluent and coherent" under cross-examination than in direct. Loren thought this was because she was not trying to please Mr. Halpern.

Bob explained to her that when court resumed, there would be an interruption in her cross-examination so he could question a psychiatrist who could appear at no other time.

"Fine," she said, "I don't mind a break."

She knew how hard Loren had worked, over the four years, to assemble a group of psychiatrists who would support the one concept vital to the success of the trial —that it was wrong for a therapist to have sex with a patient.

When the lawsuit was first started, Bob asked his brother-in-law, Dr. Alan J. Tuckman, to be their psychiatric consultant. Alan's opinion was that Dr. Hartogs' behavior was unethical, and he recommended psychiatric books that applied to the case, such as the works of Dr. Wilhelm Reich. Reich was the first psychiatrist to encourage patients to express themselves sexually in the presence of the therapist, and he coined the phrase "sexual revolution." But never did he suggest sex between patient and therapist.

Loren learned that Sandor Ferenczi, one of Freud's disciples, once showed what he thought innocent affection to patients, kissing them and letting them kiss him. Freud warned him against this, saying that any sexual intimacy between therapist and patient was "an overthrow for the cure."

A month after the summons was served on Dr. Hartogs, Loren wrote to Dr. Charles Clay Dahlberg, author of a paper, "Sexual Contact Between Patient and Therapist." It had appeared, after a number of journals turned it down as a hot potato, in *Contemporary Psychoanalysis,* 1970, Volume 6, Number 2.

In his letter Loren suggested to Dr. Dahlberg that they meet and talk about Julie's case. Dr. Dahlberg phoned and said he did not want to get involved, though he was sympathetic to the moral issue.

"Please meet Julie once," Loren pleaded. "Then if you still feel you don't want to get involved, I won't bother you anymore." He told Dr. Dahlberg he would be compensated for his time.

Dr. Dahlberg consented to see her and, after one meeting, offered to testify. From then on, Dr. Dahlberg acted, in Loren's words, as "our psychiatric keel." He suggested the names of other experts, gave them the glossary of the American Psychiatric Association, which defined psychiatric terms, and aided in the selection of the jury.

Loren wrote the district branch of the American Psychiatric Association to ask for its code of ethics. An official replied three months later that the APA had no separate code of ethics but subscribed to the American Medical Association's code. But before the trial date was set, the APA took a clear stand on the question of sex between psychiatrist and patient: "unethical."

Loren also wrote to Dr. Schneck, who consented to testify, and Dr. Anderson, who was reluctant to appear in court. Loren asked Dr. Anderson for an evaluation of Julie, and on August 5, 1972, with Julie's permission, she sent the following.

I first met Miss Julie Roy in the late spring or early summer of 1968. She was referred to me by A., a friend of hers and a patient of mine. Miss Roy was very self-conscious, very mannered, very anxious during this first interview. Although there were no psychotic symptoms apparent, viz., no indications of hallucinatory or delusional experiences, she was extremely circumstantial and tangential. It was almost impossible to obtain even the most elementary facts about her early life history, not even, as I recall, her date of birth. Furthermore, her current life, by any usual standards, seemed very strange, withdrawn, empty and isolated. The only exceptions were her friendship with A. and the fact that she was able to maintain herself on a job.

She said her "tentative diagnostic impression" was "that of latent schizophrenia with paranoid ideation." She went on:

I had been taking some post-doctoral courses
with Dr. Renatus Hartogs, under the auspices of
a psychoanalytic training center then known as the
Institute for Practicing Psychotherapists, including
courses in the diagnosis and treatment of schizophrenia. I therefore referred Miss Roy to him
thinking that he could provide not only the requisite expertise but also the objectivity which, because of my relationship with A., Miss Roy probably could not believe of me.

I neither saw nor heard anything more of her
until somewhat over two years later when, in late
September (1970) I received a phone call from
her. She sounded so terribly upset that I offered
her an appointment for that very afternoon, although it is far from my usual practice to see patients on Sundays. It was then that I learned that
she had accepted my referral to Dr. Hartogs, that
he had taken her into treatment and, according to
her, into bed.

Dr. Anderson described her sessions with Julie in
the winter of 1970 and spring of 1971. She concluded
her report: "On the basis of my brief encounter with
Miss Roy in therapy, I believe my original diagnostic
impression to be correct."

Dr. Dahlberg gave Loren the names of several psychiatrists who he thought might be willing to appear in
court, including Dr. Alfred M. Freedman of New York,
then president of the American Psychiatric Association;
Dr. Judd Marmor of Los Angeles, then president-elect;
and Dr. Francis Braceland, a former president, who was
chairman of the planning board of the Institute of Liv-

ing in Hartford, Connecticut. Dr. Freedman never answered Loren's letter, Dr. Marmor said he did not have the time to travel from California, and Dr. Braceland said he had given up appearing in courtrooms thirty years ago. Dr. Dahlberg next suggested Dr. Paul Chodoff in Washington, D.C. Dr. Chodoff agreed to testify.

Loren wrote to the Commission on Judicial Action of the American Psychiatric Association, asking it to furnish an expert witness. Dr. Alan A. Stone, chairman of the commission, replied that the policy of the organization was to refer such matters to the district branch of the APA where the therapist involved in litigation lived. Loren wrote the district branch but never received a reply.

Dr. Dahlberg happened to hear Dr. Willard Gaylin lecture on medical ethics and called Loren, suggesting Dr. Gaylin as an expert witness. Loren wrote Dr. Gaylin, who agreed to testify without compensation, even though he had never before been willing to testify at a trial.

On the last adjournment of the case, from February 24 to March 6, 1975, Loren lost Dr. Chodoff. Because of the many postponements, he said, he had canceled patients' hours too often. He suggested in his place Dr. Leon Salzman, a former Washington, D.C., psychiatrist, who now lived in New York. Dr. Salzman agreed to appear.

Loren wanted to keep the testifying psychiatrists "pristine"; he thought their impact would be greater if they appeared without knowing much about Julie or the case. He also wanted them to refute the idea that "it takes two to tango." Even lawyers were saying of her,

"She's a grown women, she knew what she was doing, why didn't she just say no?" The expert witnesses had to explain to judge and jury, "The patient may want to tango but it is up to the psychiatrist to refuse to dance."

The psychiatrists would be asked to explain the nature of transference and to describe such concepts as schizophrenia, psychotic episode, and delusion in layman's terms. Dr. Brinitzer, Dr. Hartogs' one expert, had talked with Julie for one hour and later examined her deposition, the hospital records, and reports by Dr. Anderson and Dr. Schneck. Dr. Brinitzer wrote in his report of April 23, 1973:

> This woman is a schizophrenic of the catatonic, withdrawn type. Her history indicates that against a background of a severely disturbed personality of a schizoid type, she developed schizophrenic symptoms in adolescence and adulthood leading to two hospitalizations in 1971 and the indicated treatment. She has been suffering from this slowly progressive disease for many years. . . . It is my opinion that her contact with Dr. Hartogs was not causally connected with her condition.

Bob and Loren knew from their reading that schizophrenia does not always get progressively worse. In some cases it stabilizes; in others, total remission occurs. They wanted experts who would testify to this, refuting Dr. Brinitzer's claim.

When court reconvened at two o'clock, Judge Myers announced, "We are going to take a witness out of turn now. He is a doctor who has to get away."

Dr. Gaylin took the stand. He first testified to his credentials: He was clinical professor of psychiatry at Columbia Medical School, College of Physicians and Surgeons; adjunct professor of psychiatry and law at Columbia University Law School; adjunct professor of psychiatry at Union Theological Seminary; president of the Institute of Society Ethics and the Life Sciences; and training and supervising psychoanalyst at Columbia University's Psychoanalytic Clinic for Training and Research. He estimated he had written forty to fifty articles and six books, one of which, *Teaching Medical Ethics,* was a standard textbook for medical schools. He said, "My field is primarily the uses of psychiatry to solve social problems, and I am probably best known as a psychiatric educator."

Cohen asked whether the American Psychiatric Association had adopted any rules and regulations "addressing themselves to sex between a psychiatrist and his patient."

"Yes, they have," said Dr. Gaylin.

"What position does the American Psychiatric Association take?"

Halpern rose to object and Judge Myers said, "I will sustain the objection right now." Because Dr. Gaylin was not appearing as an official of the APA, he could not present the group's viewpoint, only his own.

Then, addressing Dr. Gaylin, the judge said, "I would like to know from you, doctor, whether there is any part of the psychiatric profession that recognizes sexual intercourse between a psychiatrist and his patient as clinically, medically justified under certain circumstances?"

"To my knowledge, within the organized field of

psychiatry, there is none," said Dr. Gaylin. "If anything, there is specific interdiction that this is not an operation of a psychiatrist."

The judge asked, "And you say that is the accepted standard of psychiatrists in this community, New York City?"

"Yes," said Dr. Gaylin. "The reason I place such importance on that is normally the codes of ethics are very vague. They say things like, 'Don't do any harm. Do good. Respect your patients.' The American Medical Association code has some specific suggestions and a lot of vague ones. The American Psychiatric Association, rather than outlining its own code, took the general one for all doctors and then, because it did not want to leave this in the air, very specifically it said that this is not a matter of individual judgment. This, unequivocally, no question, is not to be done."

"Under any circumstances?" the judge asked.

"Under any circumstances. The association makes no exceptions. It wants it clearly understood that this is not to be left to the judgment of the individual psychiatrist."

Cohen asked, "Doctor, could you tell us why you feel the way you do concerning sex between a patient and his or her psychiatrist?"

"Without using technical language, I think it is easier to understand an assumption. When somebody is ill, he places exceptionally large trust in his doctor—so much so that, whether we are talking about money or sex or anything else, a doctor has a responsibility not to take advantage of a frightened and helpless patient. This is true of all medicine, not just psychiatry.

"I teach young psychiatrists in training, and I would

say the big part of training them how to be a good doctor is to help them recognize those feelings which are called by the technical name of 'transference,' which have nothing to do with the doctor. My patient may think I'm terribly handsome or wise, when I am not. These are called 'transference phenomena.' Psychiatric training recognizes that doctors, like anybody else, are vulnerable. They can be greedy. They can be very lustful. They can be immoral.

"Therefore, often the biggest part of training for a young psychiatrist is to recognize these temptations within himself, and to resist them."

Cohen asked Dr. Gaylin to explain how transference worked and what effect it had on patients.

"It means that a patient who puts his life or health in the hands of a doctor wants to think that the doctor has all the answers, and therefore, the patient is inclined to suspend his normal judgments in favor of the doctor's judgment."

"And does the concept of transference generally work as an anesthesia or a drug?"

"Not in the sense of altering consciousness. It is assumed to affect judgment," said Dr. Gaylin.

Halpern said, "I ask that answer be stricken out as not responsive, since anesthesia has nothing to do with judgment."

"I will strike the answer and ask the jury to disregard it," said the judge. "Objection sustained." Then he said to Dr. Gaylin, "You have explained, it seems to me, very eloquently and lucidly, the relationship between the doctor and his patient. But we want to know whether transference is really something like hypnotism, like putting somebody in a trance, or like a drug or an anesthesia which puts somebody out and they can't feel any pain. Is that what transference is?"

"You are giving a number of examples and as doctors, we work differently," said Dr. Gaylin. "But take the ones you used. Like an anesthesia? No. Like hypnotism? That is a fairly good analogy."

The judge asked, "Would you say a person is hypnotized?"

"In a sense, you can say that he is. Psychiatrists know there is a normal suggestibility. Hypnotism is, to us, an extreme suggestibility. We know on one level there is a suggestibility just because you are a doctor. We know that an ongoing psychiatric relationship intensifies that suggestibility."

Cohen asked, "Assuming a person is quite depressed, crying, wears the same dress for a period of a year, has difficulty starting social contact with men or women, is experiencing guilt as a result of a homosexual relationship, and assuming this person seeks a psychiatrist's assistance, can you comment on that type of person's ability to succumb to the psychiatric concept of transference?"

"I don't like being in a position of judging someone I haven't seen," said Dr. Gaylin. "But the sicker the person, the more vulnerable."

Cohen asked Dr. Gaylin to explain "countertransference."

"Countertransference means that, just as the patient is going to have feelings that aren't really appropriate to the therapy, the therapist has to be honest enough with himself to know that he too has emotions which might be destructive or not to the best interest of his patient—he is under oath to do no harm to his patient.

It means a therapist can be sexually excited by his patient but that he cannot act on his emotions, they have no place in therapy."

Cohen asked what a psychiatrist should do if he felt sexually atttracted to his patient.

Dr. Gaylin said he had two choices. "He can control the sexual attraction and not burden his patient with the knowledge of it. Or, if he feels he is falling in love with the patient, he refers the case to another psychiatrist for treatment and gives his sexual feelings priority over his therapeutic feelings. She then is no longer his patient and he is free to behave as any other human being."

Cohen asked, "Is it a commonly acceptable practice for a psychiatrist to employ a patient after therapy sessions for the purpose of typing letters or doing stenographic work?"

"No, it is not," said Dr. Gaylin.

"Can you tell us why?"

"That would go back to the heart of transference. You have to lean over backward not to take advantage of the patient when you have a feeling that he is clearly not as free in his judgments as he would be if he weren't a patient of yours. So you don't make contracts with them."

Cohen asked Dr. Gaylin to describe what harmful effects could occur if a psychiatrist had sex with a patient.

Dr. Gaylin said, "It can be destructive, because the therapeutic relationship is presumed to be nonsexual. The patient is one who has confusion about life in general, what is right and what is wrong, and often doesn't know where he is going. Having sex with a psychiatrist can cause the same kind of feeling as having sex with a parent. It is terribly destructive and dissociative, it can make your boundaries of right and wrong become terribly confused."

"Could it have an effect, doctor, on the patient's sexuality?"

"Yes, it could."

"Could you tell us how?"

"In the same way that any inappropriate sexuality, or to use the example that I used, premature sexuality or sexuality with a parent, can make all sex seem evil or dirty or terrifying."

Cohen asked if a patient-psychiatrist relationship could exist if the patient were not paying for therapy. Dr. Gaylin said he did not think it could, though there was a school of thought that believed it could. He estimated that the fees for a psychiatrist in the New York area ranged from $30 to $100 an hour, and said it was "not common" for the therapy to take only ten or fifteen minutes.

Cohen asked if sex with a psychiatrist would affect a patient's future therapeutic relationships. Dr. Gaylin said yes. He added that it could not only make the termination of treatment "much more painful," but "make trust in the next psychiatrist impossible." Dr. Gaylin also said that a psychiatrist who had seen a patient for nineteen months had a "moral responsibility" either to take care of the patient himself or refer the patient to someone else.

Under cross-examination by Halpern, Dr. Gaylin stated he had not met Julie Roy before the trial and had not asked a fee for testifying, adding, "I heard that the patient didn't have much money."

Halpern asked, "Haven't you had experience with good psychiatrists who charge ten dollars a visit, twice a week, for patients who can't pay more?"

Dr. Gaylin replied, "Not recently, unfortunately. I have not been able to place a patient for less than thirty-five dollars among students in the past five years."

"You don't know anything about the treatment that was given by Dr. Hartogs, do you?"

"Not much, no."

"You wouldn't say the treatment depends upon the amount that was paid to him as a fee?"

"I'm not sure what you mean."

"If you pay more money, you get better treatment?"

"I don't think that is necessarily so."

"You can have very good treatment by a very good man who would charge less, isn't that true?"

"Yes."

Halpern asked Dr. Gaylin what "hallucination" meant.

"Hallucination is faulty vision perception, or auditory perception. It is usually visual—seeing something that is not there."

"In other words, something that is not a reality, is that right?"

"Yes, that is correct."

"Does the person having this hallucination actually believe that it is a reality?"

"Yes, by definition."

Neither Halpern nor Cohen had further questions, so Dr. Gaylin was excused. Halpern resumed his cross-examination of Julie. Referring to the time she terminated the treatment, he said, "When Dr. Hartogs rejected your advances to him, in September of 1970, that made you feel pretty sore, didn't it?"

Cohen said, "I object to the form of that question."

"Sustained," said the judge.

Halpern withdrew the question and asked, "In September of 1970, did Dr. Hartogs say to you that he didn't want to use your services anymore?"

"I don't remember him saying that, no."

"That made you pretty mad at him, didn't it?"

"You asked her that once before," said the judge. "She said, "I was not mad. I felt betrayed.' "

" 'Felt betrayed,' " repeated Halpern. He then asked, "Was it at that time you made up your mind to sue Dr. Hartogs?"

"No," she said.

"When did you make up your mind?"

"I believe it was in January of 1972."

"And before that you had no intention of suing him?"

"Objection to that," said Cohen.

"Objection is overruled," said the judge.

"I didn't know anything about suing doctors," she said.

"Well, who told you about it, then, if you didn't know anything about it?" he asked.

"Now the objection is sustained," said the judge. "Let's not go into this phase of it. The jury will disregard this part of the testimony as to who suggested that she sue."

Halpern said, "Now, Miss Roy, I would like you to look at this list of checks."

The judge commented, "It is not a list. It is a little package."

Halpern amended, "This little pack of forty-four

checks. I ask you to look at them and tell me whether they represent checks received by you from Dr. Hartogs for typing done between November 15, 1969, and October 26, 1970."

She looked over the checks. Halpern asked, "What do they represent?"

"Some of the money Dr. Hartogs paid me for typing letters for him."

"Was that at the rate of three dollars per letter?"

"Yes," she said.

Halpern asked that the checks be marked in evidence.

Bob later told her Halpern wanted to show she had made money from Dr. Hartogs, thus minimizing the damages. The checks totaled $2835, which represented 945 letters in a time span of less than one year. As Bob had brought out earlier, these letters were written in behalf of young men who did not want to serve in Vietnam.

Cohen wanted to ask questions in redirect examination, which would give him the chance to allow Julie to explain more fully some of the points Halpern had raised, or open up other topics. He brought up the letters she had written to Dr. Hartogs during her treatment, and asked if she had any discussions with Dr. Hartogs before she sent the letters or after. She said they never discussed the letters, nor did she know whether he kept them in his file.

Halpern had a last question under recross-examination. He asked Julie, "You said that Dr. Hartogs said to you to write him letters, it would make it easier for you to express yourself, is that right?"

"Yes," she said.

"Well, was it hard to express yourself when you wrote him letters saying, 'I love you'? Isn't that what you wrote to him?"

"I don't remember what I wrote to him," she said.

At this point, late in the afternoon, the judge dismissed the jury until the following morning at ten o'clock.

Earlier that afternoon Nick Lewin, who was in the courthouse for another trial, had stopped in to watch. Julie knew Nick only slightly from the office, but his presence in the front row next to her was like that of a friend. Nick stayed through Dr. Gaylin's testimony, whispered quick explanations of what was happening at the bench when the attorneys all seemed to be talking at once to the judge, and then listened to the end of her cross-examination. She heard him tell Bob he was amazed that she seemed so "composed" throughout what, he said, had to be a harrowing experience.

In the taxi uptown, and then at the office, Bob and Loren were wondering once again whether Dr. Hartogs would appear. Bob was preparing questions for the next day's psychiatric witnesses, who could personally testify to Julie's breakdowns. He wanted them to stress the points Dr. Gaylin had made, most importantly that sex between therapist and patient was disastrous to the patient. For their case to succeed, the jury had to accept that concept, plus the truth of her story.

7

On the next day, Wednesday, March 12, the small courtroom was overflowing with people who had read about the trial in articles by Sheila Moran of the *New York Post,* the only reporter to have been there from the start. Now Donald Flynn of the *Daily News* and several other reporters also attended. There were about one hundred onlookers, mostly women. Not a seat was vacant, and some spectators stood at the rear.

Dr. Schneck was the first witness. He testified he was clinical assistant professor of psychiatry at New York Medical College; on the teaching staff at Metropolitan Hospital, where he was chief of one of the psychiatric wards; clinical associate professor of psychiatry at New Jersey Medical School; and chief of the psychiatry service at the Veterans Hospital in East Orange, New Jersey.

He told how he had first seen Julie at Metropolitan Hospital when she was mute, where her diagnosis was schizophrenia "with elements of conversion reaction or hysteria." After she left the hospital, he treated her for a year, seeing her once a week with extra sessions at times. He charged $25 a session, and each lasted forty-five minutes.

In the fall of 1971, he said, he became concerned about a "suicidal hazard" as she "expressed complete despair, saw no point in living, talked about wanting to commit suicide, about possibly buying a gun." One day in November she was "functioning so poorly" that he canceled the rest of his appointments and took her to Metropolitan for a second stay.

Dr. Schneck said he thought Julie had gone through two "psychotic episodes," each of which brought her to the hospital. He defined psychosis as "a very serious mental disturbance." He explained, "Usually it carries with it a breakdown in one's usual means of dealing with life, to the point where one can no longer manage the requirements and activities of daily living."

Cohen asked if Dr. Schneck had formed an opinion as to the causes of Julie's admissions to the hospital. Dr. Schneck said he believed Julie "had the illness called schizophrenia, an illness of a long-standing, sometimes chronic nature." He added that "one may have this illness in mild, moderate, or severe degrees, and it will wax and wane in intensity, depending on what stresses one encounters."

Dr. Schneck declared that Julie "had a troubled life from her earliest years and certainly a troubled adolescence and period in her twenties, characterized by many difficulties in living often found in people suffering from schizophrenia. Problems about establishing and maintaining relationships. Problems about serious depressions. Problems about feeling worthless. Problems of coping in general."

He said Julie told him she had consulted Dr. Hartogs and during the course of her treatment "developed romantic feelings with him and also had sexual liaison with him, which increased her feelings of dependency on him, closeness with him, and then was terminated with a rather devastating result to her."

Julie told him, he said, she often had two feelings during her sexual activities with Dr. Hartogs. "When she was feeling romantically involved with him, these were positive experiences," he said. "However, other times she felt degraded, as if she was being used, and the net result of the termination of treatment was a strong sense of betrayal on her part, a severe sense of shame and embarrassment, a tremendous injury to her own regard for herself." These feelings intensified her depression, he added.

Following the end of her therapy with Dr. Hartogs, Dr. Schneck said, Julie was "troubled by these very powerful and very painful emotions." He described the lawsuit as one attempt she made to reestablish her respect for herself and to bring about a conclusion to the therapy "that she could live with."

Dr. Schneck described Julie in his office as spending "a fair amount of time holding her arms and just rocking silently to herself, looking very, very distressed." She remained in a state of serious emotional disorder, wearing the same dress every day, though, he added, "she was meticulously neat and washed it every night."

Julie wished she could interrupt to thank Dr. Schneck for mentioning this. He could simply have said she wore the same dress month after month, and everyone would think how filthy she must have been. This man's kindness had always been there, she realized; the fact that he was a psychiatrist had made it hard for her to see it before.

Judge Myers was asking Dr. Schneck to define schizophrenia. He said there were about nine different subtypes of schizophrenia, "a major mental disturbance characterized by problems in organizing one's thoughts. It causes problems at times in perceiving the outside world—one may have hallucinations, for instance. Also problems in controlling one's feelings, so that a schizophrenic person is prone to excessive feeling changes, particularly, in this case, depressive feelings." There may also be trouble in the use of the body "so that one may find it difficult, as if walking through mud, to move one's limbs."

A person could recover from an acute psychotic episode and function quite well, he said, or he might have another psychotic episode sometime in the future. Or he might never quite recover from his first psychotic episode. In the extreme course of schizophrenia, the person never recovers but has to remain hospitalized for the rest of his life, he said, adding, "That's an unusual direction for it to take these days."

Cohen asked Dr. Schneck if he thought Julie improved while seeing him in his office. He said that before she terminated the therapy, "she was less depressed, she was displaying a great deal of anger, and had less of these major disturbances of thinking and of being able to move and carry out some of her activities. She was not suicidal at that point, and therapy ended with some improvement in that regard. She was not psychotic at the time treatment ended." He said she had never hallucinated.

Cohen asked, "Doctor, have you, in your practice, found that your female patients fell in love with you?"

"From time to time I would say a small percentage would."

"Doctor, is there a psychological term to describe the

affection that a female patient might have with you as her psychiatrist?"

"The general term used in this regard is 'transference.' " Dr. Schneck gave his definition of transference as "the phenomenon in which a patient projects onto the therapist attitudes and feelings which that person previously had for other people in their life, such as for parents." He said that this emotional reaction occurs beyond the rational control of the patient.

He explained that psychotherapy was a process carried on with words: "The transference feelings are discussed, clarified, interpreted with the patient by the use of verbal techniques. An attempt is made, always, to help the patient understand what he is experiencing, why it is happening, how it is not really appropriate in the present-day situation, what its origins were. The goal is to help the patient resolve some of the conflicts which he has carried from childhood on."

Cohen asked if Julie Roy, by virtue of her condition, was particularly sensitive to transference, and Dr. Schneck said yes. He explained that the schizophrenic patient transfers to the psychiatrist "intense feelings of love, intense feelings of hatred, intense feelings of awe and respect, and intense feelings of disdain—whatever the feelings are, they are likely to be particularly intense."

During a five-minute recess before Dr. Schneck's cross-examination, Sheila Moran walked up to Cohen and handed him a sealed letter addressed to Julie Roy. When the trial continued, Halpern objected to a reporter's giving "information" to the opposition. The judge asked Cohen to tell what had occurred.

Cohen explained, "The reporter told me she had

received a letter which she was asked to deliver to me, and she delivered it to me. I read it, and I gave it to my client to hold for me because I didn't want to put it with my litigation papers."

"You didn't discuss this case with the reporter, did you?" asked the judge.

"Your Honor, I have consistently abided with your admonition at the beginning of this trial about talking with the press," said Cohen.

The judge explained that his injunction prevented the attorneys from discussing the trial with the media, but did not prevent the media from delivering a letter to the attorneys, and Halpern's objection was overruled.

Halpern then questioned Dr. Schneck about Julie Roy's functioning on her job when she returned to work. Dr. Schneck said she did very poorly, that often she either did not go to work or went home at noon and retreated to bed.

"Doctor, did she give you a history of lesbianism?" Halpern asked.

"Homosexuality, yes," said Dr. Schneck.

"I am talking specifically about lesbianism," said Halpern.

"It's not an official term," said Dr. Schneck.

"Is it synonymous?" asked Halpern.

The judge asked, "Why go into it?"

"I want the public to know what we are talking about," said Halpern.

"They all know what we are talking about, believe me," said the judge.

Cohen asked, in his redirect examination, whether Julie had ever described to Dr. Schneck "a heterosexual relationship with Dr. Hartogs."

"She told me it had occurred," he said.

The judge announced a luncheon recess.

Bob told her, as they drank coffee, that Dr. Schneck's testimony had been right on the beam; he showed that her hospitalizations were a result of "psychotic episodes" caused by her experience with Dr. Hartogs.

They were all excited about the letter Shelia Moran had handed Bob. It had been sent to Sheila at the *Post* by a young woman, Judith Cuttler, who had read about the trial in the newspaper.

Julie went into the ladies' room to read the letter, four pages long. It described an experience with Dr. Hartogs similar to her own, except that Miss Cuttler had not given in to Dr. Hartogs' urging that she have sex with him. Miss Cuttler also mentioned the way he would say, "Next question," when she was telling him her problems.

Julie felt sad and angry reading the letter, and she realized Miss Cuttler had probably felt the same when she read newspaper accounts of Julie's testimony. Julie was touched that Miss Cuttler addressed her as "Dear sister." The letter went on to say Miss Cuttler would do anything she could to help, even testify. But did she mean it? A number of other women had called Bob with similar stories saying they would do "anything" to help, but when it came down to it, they meant "anything but testify." Still, the letter gave Julie moral support, and she silently thanked Miss Cuttler for her courage.

As the afternoon session opened there came another moment of drama. Halpern announced Dr. Hartogs would appear in court as a witness in his own defense.

Cohen asked the judge for permission, as was his right, to question Dr. Hartogs before he testified.

The judge said he would allow this "provided it doesn't unduly prolong the trial." He set the deposition for the following afternoon, and the trial proceeded with the calling of the third psychiatric expert.

Dr. Leon Salzman testified he was professor of clinical psychiatry at Albert Einstein Medical School; faculty member of the William Alanson White Institute; professor at Tulane University Medical School in New Orleans; and deputy director and clinical director of the Bronx Psychiatric Center. Author of four books and more than a hundred articles in the field of psychiatry, he described much of his work as dealing with "the problems of sex in terms of therapeutic processes and in terms of the development of personality."

Dr. Salzman agreed with Dr. Schneck's definition of schizophrenia, saying it was not a specific illness "but a sort of basket in which a great many disorders are placed." He said it was very common for a schizophrenic breakdown to be caused by a traumatic situation.

Cohen asked, "Now, doctor, do you have an opinion as to whether it is acceptable under standard medical practices in New York for a psychiatrist to have sex with his patient or her patient?"

"I certainly do," said Dr. Salzman.

"Could you tell us, please, what that opinion is?"

"I think that it can never, never be justified as part of the therapeutic program in the treatment of mental illness of any kind."

He stated that because the nature of the relationship of psychiatrist and patient is one of trust, the quality of the relationship is destroyed when sexual relations take place. He agreed with Dr. Schneck that because patients suffering from schizophrenia were "the people who have the least hold on reality," a sexual relationship with such a patient was "the most destructive kind of intervention."

Dr. Salzman also agreed with Dr. Schneck that sex between therapist and patient could produce "a schizophrenic episode."

Cohen asked if the payment of money was necessary for the existence of a patient-psychiatrist relationship, and Dr. Salzman said no.

In cross-examination, Halpern asked Dr. Salzman to define "delusion," and Dr. Salzman described it as "a false belief."

Halpern asked, "While she is hallucinating, does she actually believe what she is hallucinating is reality?"

"Yes, and no, because in one part of her mind she does, in another part she does not."

"Well, doctor, did you ever open the mind of a patient to realize that?" asked Halpern.

"Yes, that's what we do all the time," said Dr. Salzman.

"Are you referring to a lobotomy?"

"I am referring to the process of psychotherapy. It is an attempt to open the mind of people to understand what goes on inside."

"Doctor, did you ever have a lobotomy performed on any of your patients?"

"No, sir."

The judge said to Halpern, "Why don't you stick to the question of hallucinations, which you are on?"

"I was going to come to that through lobotomy, because it was accepted practice for hallucinations," said Halpern.

"Never," said Dr. Salzman.

"Now you got your answer," said the judge to Halpern.

Halpern said, "Now, doctor, if you were to receive information that this particular patient, and we are talking about the plaintiff, used to go down to a bar, get drunk, pick up men, and in two instances take them back to either a hotel or to a motel, and if, during the time she was treated by the psychiatrist, [she] did the same thing on two occasions, and subsequent to her being treated in this nineteen-month period, did the same thing—would you say, doctor, that is rational on the part of a person who goes about her business normally?"

"Yes, I would say that is very common behavior in New York."

"Now, doctor, in addition, would it affect your opinion, if you found that she was—with the permission of my friend—" nodding at the judge, "a lesbian?"

"That's also very common."

"And had a relationship with women on several occasions? Would you say that that was normal too?"

"Homosexual behavior in both sexes is not abnormal behavior. It is behavior which is considered to be the choice of sexual partners, according to their tastes and liking."

"And there is no traumatic shock in all of these incidents of picking up people at bars and sleeping with them?"

"If you are saying that it is a shock for a woman to

go to bars and pick up men, I would say no. It is not a shock."

"Would you say that is an impulse on the part of a schizophrenic to go down to the bar and pick up these men and go through these acts?"

"Not at all," said Dr. Salzman.

Halpern asked, "How much are you getting, by the way, to come down here, doctor?"

"Five hundred dollars."

"Let me ask you another thing. Would you frown upon a psychiatrist who charged ten dollars for ten or fifteen minutes of treatment?"

"I would, because I don't consider ten minutes adequate to do psychotherapy, even if you charge nothing."

"Let me ask you this. Supposing the patient can't afford to pay any more. Would you still insist on thirty, seventy, or a hundred dollars?"

"I have treated patients who can't afford more," he said, adding, "If patients need more time, we should arrange for them to go to clinics, and not give them a so-called therapeutic time which is not therapy at all."

Cohen then called Dr. Dahlberg, associate clinical professor of psychiatry at New York University Medical Center and visiting psychiatrist at Bellevue Hospital. Dr. Dahlberg testified he had examined Julie in four sessions of at least an hour each, reviewed all her records, and concluded that her hospital admissions were caused by her "brooding intensely over a long period of time about the sexual acts that she was engaged in with Dr. Hartogs."

Cohen asked, "Doctor, do you have an opinion with respect to whether Julie Roy had a delusion or hallucination about having sex with Dr. Hartogs?"

"In my opinion there was nothing delusional about it at all. And that is consistent with all of the records that I read."

Cohen asked if Dr. Dahlberg agreed with the other expert witnesses that sex between a psychiatrist and patient was "unethical."

Dr. Dahlberg declared, "Sex with the patient is not any recognized form of therapy." He added that sometimes patients try to seduce doctors, particularly psychiatrists, and doctors had to be "above" succumbing.

In cross-examination, Halpern asked if Dr. Dahlberg believed Julie Roy was telling the truth, and he said, "Absolutely."

Calling Julie "schizophrenic," Halpern said, "Did you ask her anything with respect to her early life, say up to the time of her teens, to determine what the cause of this condition was?"

"I asked her about her childhood. But we do not know the etiology of schizophrenia."

"Well, can you tell us when the onset of this schizophrenia came about?"

"I would guess, and this is only a guess, it probably started right after her brother's suicide."

The trial was adjourned until the next morning.

Bob, Loren, and the crisis research team went into action to determine questions for Dr. Hartogs' cross-examination.

Nick Lewin had suggested that someone on the team should read everything Dr. Hartogs had written, not only the superficial columns for *Cosmopolitan* but all his medical treatises as well. Nick had got in touch with a friend of his, Bernard Witlieb, a professor of English at City University of New York who was interested in legal matters, and Mr. Witlieb had agreed to do this reading, refusing any compensation.

Now Mr. Witlieb was summoned to the office. He reported he had covered the medical libraries in the Bronx, Brooklyn, and Manhattan, as well as the New York Public Library, reading all of Dr. Hartogs' books and papers that were available. His most interesting finding, they thought, was that Dr. Hartogs had written an article saying that, in his opinion, almost all instances of male impotence were psychologically caused.

Besides his report, Mr. Witlieb brought bagels and cream cheese to the office, knowing everyone was working late and likely to be hungry. Only Julie refused to eat. All that testimony about her eating habits—some of it very much exaggerated—left her with no appetite.

Bob also prepared his questioning of the next day's witnesses: Evan Forgelman, the only person to see her on a daily basis during the troubled years, and Dr. Anderson. No one knew what Dr. Anderson would say, as Bob had had no opportunity to interview her. She had not wanted to testify, but Loren felt strongly that her absence would leave an obvious gap in the case. So she had been subpoenaed.

Julie was sorry to think of the embarrassment Dr. Anderson would feel on describing how she had referred Julie to Dr. Hartogs. But as the sixth day of the trial approached, Julie's biggest worry still was facing Dr. Hartogs himself.

8

~~~~~~~~~~~~~~~~~~~~~~~~~~~~

As Julie waited for court to reconvene on Thursday, March 13, she saw a figure enter the room wearing a dark overcoat and carrying a briefcase in each hand. She asked Loren, "Who is that?"

Loren said, "That's Dr. Hartogs."

She stared in disbelief. He was far heavier than when she had known him, and his hair had turned completely white. Where before he had been clean-shaven, he now had a full beard. His hat was pulled down to his eyes, so that not much of his face showed.

She expected him to turn on her in fury, but he seemed afraid to look at her. Without glancing her way, he took a seat at the opposite end of the front row, as far from her as he could get.

Then Evan came in and greeted her warmly. He was to be the first witness of the day, and she was delighted to see him.

Cohen called to the stand Evan Forgelman, vice-president and director of sales promotion at *Esquire*. He testified Julie Roy had worked for him nine years, first as secretary, then as his assistant, until she left of her own will in May of 1973.

He described Julie's work as "quite satisfactory" for the first four years. But in the fall of 1968 there came "a very marked change," he said. This was shown in "a wide variety of behavior." He explained, "First, Julie, who was a very prompt person in the morning, began to arrive rather late, and she left early. She would start to cry for no reason whatsoever. She seemed unable to relate to me as closely and as professionally during this period as she had in the past."

One morning in the summer of 1969, she told him she wanted to quit and asked for her paycheck, he said. He tried to talk her out of leaving but she was insistent. Several days later she returned and said she wanted her job back. After that her work became unsteady. "Whereas she performed very well on some days, she performed very poorly on other days," he said. There were times when she wore the same dress for weeks on end, other times when she arrived "very fashionably attired."

One day in September, 1970, he said, there was a "remarkable change in Julie. She came to work and began to cry hysterically." He said he had never seen her "in such a distressed emotional state," that she was "very uncommunicative." This mood, he said, continued through the summer of 1971. He thought of firing her but said he considered her emotional state comparable to a physical illness.

When Julie left *Esquire* in May, 1973, her performance on the job had improved, and she seemed to be in better control of herself, even though she was still "erratic" from time to time, he said.

The judge asked Forgelman to reconcile his observations with Julie's personnel record at *Esquire,* which noted that when she quit she had an "excellent record," and showed salary increases from $90 a week to $200.

Forgelman explained that she was a highly efficient assistant and an excellent typist who "even at fifty percent of her capacity was better than many people at eighty or ninety percent." He said he recommended the raises due her every six months as cost-of-living increases.

"When she left after nine years of a very loyal and devoted relationship, I couldn't possibly say anything other than she was excellent because I felt that her responses were emotionally derived and that she couldn't control them," he said.

Halpern asked, "In all the years that she worked at *Esquire,* did you have any knowledge that she was a lesbian?"

"Of course not. No," said Forgelman.

"Did you know that she got drunk, went down to the Village to a place called Slug's, and would pick up a man and sleep with him?"

Cohen objected to these questions as "inflammatory," and the judge sustained his objection.

Dr. Anderson had been scheduled to testify, but she was ill and could not appear until the next day. Cohen asked the judge for a conference at the bench, outside the hearing of the jury and spectators. At this time he announced he wanted to offer "several female witnesses, ex-patients of Dr. Hartogs, who will testify that during the course of their treatment with Dr. Hartogs, he prescribed sex as part of the therapy." These women, he said, had seen Dr. Hartogs at various times, from the days when he was a resident psychiatrist in Montreal up to the time he treated Julie Roy. Cohen said he would need some notice in order to bring these witnesses to court.

Halpern opposed this. He said to the judge, "You will

be trying a case within a case, trying all sorts of people. I think it is highly inflammatory."

The judge said, "I'm not going to rule on it now. I am reserving decision. It would appear to me, though, that it would be highly prejudicial to the defendant to permit testimony of this type to go in on the main case. The main case should stand or fall on this particular incident with the plaintiff herself."

He added that if Dr. Hartogs should testify that he never prescribed sexual relations as treatment, that he never had sexual relations with a patient, that he did not recognize sex as an accepted therapy "for what ailed this plaintiff," then he, the judge, would permit the other patients to testify during the rebuttal.

Then the judge told the jury a matter had to be taken care of outside their presence. This was the deposition of Dr. Hartogs, which the court had ordered.

The judge, jury, and spectators left the courtroom, leaving the stenographer, the opposing lawyers, Dr. Hartogs, and Julie. Though she sat only about ten feet from him, he still did not look at her.

Cohen asked Dr. Hartogs, "During the period between February '69 and November '69, did you ever suggest to Miss Roy, in words or substance, that she have sex with you?"

"Never," said Dr. Hartogs.

"Did you ever lie on the couch with her?"

"Never," said Dr. Hartogs.

"Did you ever expose yourself in her presence?"

"Never," said Dr. Hartogs.

Cohen asked, "Do you have any gross abnormalities on your body?"

Halpern interposed, "The answer is yes, and we refuse to answer at this time."

"Do you refuse to tell us what that is?" asked Cohen.

Halpern said, "We reserve that for examination later on. You're not entitled to that. This is not a negligence case."

"We'll find out if we're entitled to it," said Cohen.

"We'll do that," Halpern said grimly.

Cohen asked Dr. Hartogs, "How long have you had that gross abnormality?"

Halpern objected to the question.

Cohen asked, "Doctor, are you able to perform sexual acts?"

Halpern said, "What period? His age is sixty-six at the present time. Why don't you be more specific?"

"Up to 1970, doctor," said Cohen.

"No," said Dr. Hartogs.

"When were you stopped being able to have sex?"

"In '65."

"And what was the medical reason for your inability to have sex?"

Halpern objected, saying to Dr. Hartogs, "Don't answer."

Cohen said, "Let's get rulings, shall we?"

Halpern said, "Sure."

The opposing lawyers went to the chambers of Judge Myers. When they returned Cohen said, "Let the record reflect that the judge has directed Dr. Hartogs to respond to questions concerning his statement that he has a gross abnormality on the private parts of his body, and in connection with the fact that he has testified that he is impotent since 1965." Then Cohen asked Dr. Hartogs, "Doctor, what is the gross abnormality that you state you have?"

"I have a tumor on my right testicle, which I have had since I was in concentration camp. I was kicked by a guard," said Dr. Hartogs.

"And is it an enlargement on your right testicle?"

"It's a gross enlargement that anybody that has sex with me can see."

"How large is the enlargement, doctor?"

"I would say it's five or six times as large as the other one."

"And have you been treated for that in the United States?"

"I have had great discomfort from it—"

"That's not my question, doctor. Have you been treated for that in the United States?"

"I want to explain to you—"

"Yes or no?"

"No."

"Have you been admitted to any hospitals or sought any hospital treatment in connection with that?"

"Strang Clinic."

"Where is that?"

"That's on Thirty-fourth Street and Park Avenue."

"When were you admitted to Strang Clinic in connection with that?"

"I consulted with them on several occasions."

"When?"

Dr. Hartogs said, "I don't know. Throughout the years."

"Starting when, doctor? When was the first time that you went to that clinic?" said Cohen.

"You nail me down to exact dates—"

"Approximately when?"

"Approximately I went in '66, approximately I went in '70, and I went last year. In '74."

"Any other gross abnormalities, doctor?"

"No."

"Has the tumor been diagnosed at the Strang Clinic?"

"Yes."

"As benign?"

"Benign."

Cohen asked, "Doctor, in connection with your claim of impotency in 1965, what was the cause of that impotency?"

"The tumor."

"And in 1965 did you seek medical assistance?"

"Sixty-six, I think it was."

"And were you married during the period of '66 to '70?"

"Yes."

"And you had no sexual relations with your wife during that period of time?"

"No."

"And you had no sexual relations with anybody?"

"That's right."

Cohen mentioned the names of nine women who told him that while patients of Dr. Hartogs they were sexually involved with him. He asked Dr. Hartogs if these women had been his patients. Dr. Hartogs refused to answer on advice of Halpern, who said this related to confidentiality between physician and patient.

When the deposition had ended and Dr. Hartogs left with his lawyers, Bob, Loren, and Julie stared at each other in amazement.

Bob said to her, "Julie, are you sure you never noticed anything?"

"Not a thing," she said. Either this enlarged testicle was a recent development, or he had somehow concealed the swelling when he had sex with her.

On the fifth day of the trial—Friday, the fourteenth—Julie saw Dr. Hartogs enter the courtroom and take a seat with his attorneys at the counsel table. As he opened one of his briefcases, the contents spilled to the floor. She felt an impulse to rush over and pick up the papers for this pathetic-looking old man. Dr. Hartogs seemed nervous, and she felt embarrassed for him; somehow she did not want him to feel uneasy. Thinking about this later, she couldn't understand why she still cared.

The first witness called was Dr. Pauline Anderson. She testified that she had a Ph.D. in psychology from the New School for Social Research. She was a former senior psychologist for the Jewish Board of Guardians and for more than twenty years served as chief psychologist for the New York State Employment Service. Cohen asked how long she had been in private practice and she said, "On an intermittent basis since 1936, but continuously since 1966."

Dr. Anderson said that on the last or the next-to-the-last Sunday in September of 1970, Julie had called her, "very upset." She then saw Julie twice a week until the end of May, with certain gaps. She said Julie had described her sexual experiences with Dr. Hartogs.

Cohen asked if she believed Julie was "delusional."

"Absolutely not," said Dr. Anderson.

"What do you base that opinion on, doctor?"

"It is very hard to say. When you are dealing with a person who is disturbed, who says, 'My therapist had sex with me,' your first thought is, 'This may be fantasy.' So you keep an open mind. But as time goes on and the talk revolves around this, then you come to a conclusion, and I came to the conclusion that Julie Roy was not giving me fantasy but fact."

Halpern, cross-examining, asked, "You knew about Dr. Hartogs, didn't you, at that time in 1969?"

"Certainly," she said.

"As a matter of fact, you attended his lectures, didn't you?"

"Certainly."

"Did you think of him highly as a competent psychiatrist?"

"I did."

"Do you still think he is a competent psychiatrist?"

"No," she said.

"And the only reason you don't think so is because of what Julie told you?"

"Yes," she said.

Halpern asked, "Did you communicate with Dr. Hartogs at all?"

"No," she said.

"To ask him whether there was any truth in that statement?"

"No."

"Didn't you think that as a psychologist you should have?"

"No."

Under redirect examination by Cohen, Dr. Anderson said she thought that when psychiatrists advocated having sex with patients as "therapy," this was "rationalization on the part of therapists who have sexual hang-ups of their own."

After Dr. Anderson left the stand, Cohen asked the judge to direct that Dr. Hartogs submit to a physical examination by a urologist of the plaintiff's choice "to determine the organic genesis, if any, of the proposed malady" that Dr. Hartogs claimed had made him impotent. The judge granted the request.

Julie shared the relief she knew Bob and Loren felt at that moment. Dr. Anderson's sympathetic testimony had been a welcome surprise to them all, and the judge's favorable ruling on Bob's last request could prove to be a turning point. Now the main issue confronting the jurors, who had sat stone-faced throughout the trial, boiled down to: Who was telling the truth, the patient or the doctor?

The answer to that question might well depend on Dr. Hartogs' testimony.

9

The plaintiff's side had concluded its arguments. Now it was the defendant's turn. Dr. Hartogs walked to the witness stand wearing gray trousers and a dark-blue jacket, and Julie marveled at his confidence, thinking, He didn't even bother to put on a suit.

Dr. Hartogs, answering Halpern's questions, first testified as to his credentials. He reported he had earned a Ph.D. in psychology in 1932 at the University of Frankfurt-am-Main, then a Master of Medical Science degree from the Brussels Medical School in 1939. Coming to this country in 1940, he received his Master of Arts degree in clinical psychopathology in 1945, and his medical degree in 1948 from the University of Montreal Medical School. He interned at two hospitals in Montreal, Nôtre Dame and Hôtel Dieu, and his residency in psychiatry was spent at St. Jean de Dieu Hospital in Montreal in 1949 and 1950. He qualified as a psychiatrist in New York State, and was approved by the Mental Hygiene Department in 1955.

Among the positions he had held were senior psychiatrist at Sing Sing, senior psychiatrist for the probation department of the courts of New York, and associate in psychiatry and neurology at French Hospital in New York City. He was currently the medical director of the Community Guidance Service of New York City, and since 1966 had been the associate director of the American Institute for Psychotherapy and Psychoanalysis in New York. He was also the clinical supervisor and consulting psychiatrist for the Institutes of Applied Human Dynamics, centers for the multiply handicapped and children with brain disabilities.

His teaching career included posts as instructor in medical and abnormal psychology at McGill University School of Social Work; instructor in psychiatry at Columbia University, College of Physicians and Surgeons; lecturer in psychopathology and criminological psychiatry at the New York University School of Public Administration; and, currently, lecturer at the American Institute for Psychotherapy and Psychoanalysis.

Among the organizations to which he belonged were the American Medical Association, the American Psychiatric Association, the New York Society for Clinical Psychiatry, the New York Council for Child Psychiatry, the Academy of Psychosomatic Medicine, of which he was a fellow, the International Society of Criminology, the American Academy of Psychotherapists, the Society of Medical Group Psychoanalysts, the American Society of Psychoanalytic Physicians, and the American Society for Clinical Hypnosis.

Listening to his credentials, Julie was impressed all over again. Then she remembered Bob had told her the only requirement for membership in a number of these organizations was the ability to write a check for the dues.

Dr. Hartogs testified he had written the following books: *Knowledge of Human Nature; Principles of Suggestion and Autosuggestion; The Inferiority Feeling;*

How to Grow Up Successfully; The Two Assassins; Four-Letter Word Games; Violence: Its Causes and Solutions; and *Questions Women Ask*. He said he also had written many articles, including "Discipline in the Early Life of Sex Delinquents and Sex Criminals," and "a little column for *Cosmopolitan* magazine."

Halpern asked Dr. Hartogs if he had ever received any awards, and he said he was the recipient of the Distinguished Humanitarian Award of the Institutes of Applied Human Dynamics, "given to me by what is now, today, Mayor Beame."

"Now, doctor, as part of your expertise, did you have occasion in 1953 to examine Lee Harvey Oswald?" asked Halpern.

"Yes," he said.

Dr. Hartogs' book *The Two Assassins,* written with Lucy Freeman, was a psychological study of Lee Harvey Oswald and Jack Ruby. Dr. Hartogs had examined Oswald on May 1, 1953, when he was chief psychiatrist at Youth House, New York City's detention home for delinquent children. Oswald, then thirteen years old, was living in New York with his mother, and truancy had landed him in Dr. Hartog's office.

Cohen objected to the reference to Oswald, saying, "I don't see the relevance to this." The judge sustained his objection. Halpern then asked for a luncheon recess, and court was adjourned until two o'clock.

After lunch, the judge announced to the jammed courtroom, "We are going to take another witness out of turn."

Joseph DePhillips of 624 East Eighty-fifth Street, Brooklyn, was called as a witness for the defendant. He was a commercial photographer who testified that he had taken a photograph of the couch in Dr. Hartogs' office, which the defendant was claiming was too small for sexual intimacy.

Then Dr. Hartogs resumed the stand.

Julie had lost some of her fear of him, and now was waiting with curiosity to see how he would try to appeal to the judge and jury.

Halpern was asking Dr. Hartogs when he first saw Julie Roy.

Dr. Hartogs answered, "I saw Julie Roy on February 15, 1969, for the first time."

Halpern asked, "Will you tell this jury what occurred —what she said to you, what complaints she made to you, what you did at that time?"

"I asked her first about her identity and she said that she was twenty-six years old, which I found later was incorrect. I asked her further what work she was doing. She said she was a secretary-typist. I asked her where she was born. She said in Michigan, 9-8-38, and that she was divorced. I asked her for her address and her telephone number, and I asked her by whom she was referred. She said Dr. Anderson.

"I asked her about the reasons for which she came for treatment and she said that she was utterly confused, unhappy, depressed, and somewhat anxious. She could not make any go in life. She felt very lonely and threatened.

"I noted on my chart here that she was very distrustful in her relationship to me. Her answers were given very hesitantly. It took a long time for me to elicit some answers—"

The judge interrupted Dr. Hartogs to eject a spectator who was talking loudly. Then he said to Dr. Hartogs, "I am sorry, doctor."

Dr. Hartogs went on: "I noticed that her sentences were occasionally disconnected. She was incoherent. She mumbled sometimes. She sat for several sessions, and that started right away in the beginning, facing the wall to her right, not looking at me across the desk, and frequently she didn't give me any answers at all. I had to prompt her again and again in order to get some information out of her. She apparently didn't have the will to communicate. She complained also that she had ideas about people being after her."

Cohen asked, "Your Honor, is this in the first session, just so I understand?"

Dr. Hartogs said, "Yes, the first session. She said that she was phobic, that means fearful, of heights, of water, of lightning, and of thunder. While she was talking, she played with her fingers and pushed some of her hair in front of her face as if she was going to hide behind it. Occasionally, she put her fingers in her nose and in her ears."

How disgusting! Julie thought. Some lies hurt more than others.

Dr. Hartogs was saying, "I asked her if she had any dreams. She said she had frequent nightmares about 'people watching me, people trying to harm me, people want things from me.'

"I asked her about her family background. She said

that her parents were divorced when she was three years old and that she was the youngest of four children. She mentioned one brother who committed suicide at the age of thirty and two sisters.

"While she was talking, she had what we call in psychiatry 'ideas of reference,' which means that when a patient sees two people, for instance, talking to each other, she always believes that these people must be talking about her. She acknowledged ideas of reference.

"She admitted to feelings of being used by others and that those feelings started from early childhood on by a teacher. She hated her teacher. She didn't want to go to school. She had low grades.

"Then she said something very significant. She said she enjoys telling lies about people. That she has desires for retaliation and revenge. That she enjoys hurting people for injuries and insults allegedly inflicted upon her.

"I made here a note, because I wanted to explain to myself what that meant. It meant very likely that this sick person on one hand wanted to reach out for people, but was afraid of rejection, and on the other hand, hated people for being in this conflict.

"Then, at the end, she stated that she had very ambivalent feelings about her father, who neglected her physically ever since her parents were divorced, but contributed to her financial support until the age of eighteen.

"At the end of this session, it was quite clear to me that it was not a simple case of depression, but it was a case of schizophrenia, paranoid type, with catatonic features."

Halpern said, "Stop there for a moment, doctor.

Could you tell us in layman's language what 'schizophrenia, paranoid type, with catatonic features' means?"

"Yes," said Dr. Hartogs. "Schizophrenia is a very serious mental illness which is characterized by the fact that the individual finds it very difficult to survive in this world and has tremendous difficulties in dealing with himself as well as with other people. He finds it difficult to work consistently and has difficulties in thinking logically.

"And paranoid, which is a subtype of schizophrenia, relates to the fact that these individuals are preoccupied with ideas of persecution or grandiosity. In her case, it was persecution. She felt that people were doing her injustice, and these false beliefs about people and the world are called delusions.

"Catatonic refers to the fact that in addition to being schizophrenic, in addition to being paranoid, she also tends to be mute and turn away and be uncommunicative for long hours. Sometimes she was not communicative for the whole session and then at the end, when I said, 'We've arrived at the end of the session,' she was very angry.

"Sometimes she came out of this catatonic lethargy, or stupor, as we call it, and became very violent. At that moment she threw things at me that were on the table and she threw books down that were on the table. I didn't say anything. I felt this was a sick patient and I had to be understanding in order to reach some kind of contact with her."

"Now, you told us about the first visit, is that right?"

"Yes."

"Now, when did she again visit you as a patient?"

"She came back on the twenty-first of February, 1969. She was just as mute as she was before."

"What does your notation state?"

"Depression. It said, 'No change and distrustful behavior.' In order to help her along to express herself a little bit better, I gave her a prescription of Dexamyl, which is a combination of Dexedrine and a barbiturate. Usually this facilitates the communication between the patient and the doctor. And then I also gave her Triavil. Triavil is a combination of Elavil and Trilafon, which is to say a combination of an antidepressant and a tranquilizer."

"Well, on February twenty-one, 1969, did you find any evidence of depression?"

"Yes, there was depression."

"Was it simple or marked?"

"It was simple depression."

"Will you look at your notes, please, for that date?" requested Halpern.

"Yes. I would like to add something to the first session, if I may."

"No, I am asking for February twenty-one, 1969. Did you write down there, 'marked depression'?"

"It is 'marked depression,' but it was not of such a nature that she was panicky or desperate," said Dr. Hartogs. "It could be noticed, but that is not excessive."

He said that on the next session, February 28, "Patient arrived in her usual blue dress."

"What do you mean by 'usual blue dress'?" asked Halpern.

"She had only one dress, like a maternity dress, which she wore each time because she wanted to hide her obesity. And she always had a ribbon in her hair, either a blue ribbon or a pink ribbon."

"From the time you first started therapy up to ten months later, did she change that dress at all?"

"No, never."

"And how about the ribbon?"

"The ribbon sometimes changed color."

"Will you tell us what occurred on the twenty-eighth of February?"

"At that session she again sat, turned her chair around, and looked at the wall, and didn't talk for twenty minutes, although I encouraged her to say something or to talk about herself, and then I waited.

"All of a sudden, after twenty minutes, she said, 'Why don't you ask me something?' Suddenly she cried. She held her face in her hands but then she refused to talk and answer any more questions.

"At that time, in order to see if I could reach her, I held my hand over the table and asked her, 'Could you shake hands with me?' This is an acceptable psychiatric procedure. She ignored my hand and said, 'I cannot.'

"And then suddenly she stood up, threw the check on the table, and left, and then came back and asked for an appointment. We made some arrangement that I would see her twice weekly, each time for ten dollars, although my usual fee is sixty dollars and eighty dollars and one hundred dollars. But she claimed that she was very poor and I always make concessions. I see patients also for nothing. But in her case, she agreed that she would be able to pay ten dollars."

He said he saw on the average twelve to fourteen patients a day, six days a week, adding, "On some days I will see many more." The next time he had seen Julie was March 7, when "she seemed to be in a better mood, but in a fairly silly way of reacting. She laughed without any provocation. Then she stated that one of her lesbian friends wanted to visit her but that she refused to see this lesbian friend."

Halpern asked, "Doctor, up to this point, were you aware that she was a lesbian?"

"Yes, that's what I wanted to say about the first session, because she told me that she was a lesbian, that she hated men, that she was married for a few years—I think four or five—hated her husband, that she wasn't interested in games, no sports, that she had no friends, that she worked in an ice cream parlor where she would eat ice cream constantly in huge quantities, she left the ice cream parlor because she had arguments with other employees, and that she engaged in drinking. She lived in Chicago for five years and then came to New York at the age of twenty-five and had sporadic affairs with other lesbians."

"When did you see her next, doctor?"

"On March fourteenth."

"What transpired at that time?"

"She maintained the old rigid attitude and didn't talk at all."

"What do you mean by 'rigid attitude'?"

"Sitting up like this," he sat straight in the chair, "and looking at the wall, ignoring me completely."

On the twenty-first, he said, "Patient came in and was quite furious at me for not making her talk in the last session. While she was talking to me, she became more and more angry and accused me of wanting to sabotage her treatment. So here, all of a sudden, she could not control her hate, and the real anger of which she was capable became apparent. I decided to give her a prescription for Thorazine, fifty milligrams, Stelazine, and Cogentin."

"Tell us what these drugs are used for."

"Thorazine is a tranquilizer which is used for the treatment of schizophrenics who are in a state of psychotic agitation. Stelazine is used in order to minimize the anger or the anxiety of the psychotic patient, and Cogentin is used in order to eliminate any undesirable side effects of these two aforementioned drugs."

He said he had next seen Julie on March 23, two days later, and "she didn't seem to be angry. But she admitted that the evening before she was very depressed and she took what she called an overdose of aspirin. I asked her how many aspirin tablets did she take. She didn't know. She just felt that she took too many in order to calm herself down."

Halpern asked, "Now, doctor, in these few sessions that you talked to us about, did she show any inclination of liking you?"

"No. Not at all. She hated me and she continued to hate me until the last day of her treatment."

Halpern questioned him about the next two sessions. Dr. Hartogs, consulting his notes, said that she had been uncooperative on both occasions.

On the tenth of April "she complained about having eaten two pints of ice cream and she wanted some medication to curb her appetite. As I had some samples of Preludin, I gave her six Preludins."

"When she came to you in February, 1969, what did she weigh?" Halpern asked.

"I have no scale. But she must have weighed at least a hundred eighty or a hundred eighty-five pounds."

Never! Julie's mind screamed. Can anyone here imagine me that gross? She would always be grateful to Sheila Moran for the tactful way she first described Julie in the *New York Post:* "amply proportioned."

He said that on the twenty-fourth of April, "I asked her, 'Could we talk about your childhood?' She became immediately angry and said that she didn't want me investigating her childhood. She talked rather about a married girl friend in New York City to whom she felt attracted, and with whom she, however, can't—she used the word 'proliferate.' I thought that this was another word for getting along with somebody. We find that in schizophrenics—a strange use of language."

"Proliferate"? This was news to her. She was finding Dr. Hartogs' testimony even more interesting than she had expected.

On May first, Dr. Hartogs read from his notes, "Patient was again mute. She didn't talk. Then she responded to some questioning about what she did and how she felt and where she had been, how the work was. These are the usual questions. And then all of a sudden she asked me whether she could receive some protection against people from the underworld. I asked her, 'What do you mean by this?' She could not amplify."

Halpern asked, "Is that symptomatic, doctor, of a schizophrenic?"

"Yes, paranoid type," Dr. Hartogs said.

He next saw her on May 4, when "she was very angry and hostile. She states that she hates all men and that she doesn't like me, her therapist. But I said to her, 'Why don't you change?' and she said she doesn't want to change, and that was the end of her talking. I felt that she was a little bit tense and nervous and gave her a prescription for Librax, a tranquilizer that calms the individual down, for five tablets."

He discussed the next five visits, describing her as "distrustful," "angry," "not talkative." On June 2, he said, "she didn't even wait for the half hour to pass, and she walked out after twenty minutes."

"She walked out in a nice quiet way, doctor?"

"No, at a given moment she would all of a sudden get up, throw the check—she always paid—on the table or on the floor, and walk out."

She remembered doing that a few times—and not just throwing the check on the desk, but crumpling it up in a little ball too. She was always surprised when he was able to cash such checks. But it would make her so mad when he cut a session short!

On June 15, Dr. Hartogs said, "She talked during the whole session about lesbians she had known in the past and about a young woman she claimed she had picked up the day or two days before. I asked her what kind of a woman, and she said an attractive young woman and that she was able to talk with her. I asked her what they would talk about, but she could not say."

Julie recalled the incident. He had urged her to make up a sexual fantasy about a woman. So she did. The story involved a potter she supposedly met in Washington Square and spent the weekend with. Now he is the one having trouble separating fact from fantasy, she thought.

Dr. Hartogs said that on the twenty-second of June, "Patient came in smiling and she was coquettish. She walked in a somewhat affected way. We talked about the change in her attitude toward me. She said she was somewhat friendlier but she said that her thinking was still not what she wanted it to be. It was still constructed in a way which was foreign to her."

"What do you mean, doctor, it 'was foreign to her'?" asked Halpern.

"The thoughts she had appeared strange to her, as if they were not her thoughts." He said this was a "manifestation of schizophrenia in general, people feel influenced in their thinking by other forces."

On July 21, he said, consulting his notes, "Here she complained that she was not able to manage financially. She said that life provided too much stress for her. And then we talked about life and the world and she called the world 'syrupy.' I asked her to explain but she could not."

On July 28, he said, "Patient was depressed and she complained about intestinal cramps. I gave her another tranquilizer, Valium, and Chardonna. Chardonna is a combination of charcoal, which absorbs the gases in the intestinal tract, and belladonna, which soothes the violent constrictions of the intestine.

"But at that time she came out with something very tragedic and horrendous. She confided to me that she

wanted to stop working, take all her money from the
bank, and go to the Grand Canyon and kill herself.

"At that moment I realized the danger in which she
was and I asked her, 'How much money do you have
in order to finance such a trip?'" and she said four hundred dollars. I said, "Look here, you have to take the
money from the bank and give it to me for your own
protection, because you have things to live for. We will
try very hard to help you and you don't have to kill
yourself.'

"Why did she choose the Grand Canyon? Because
she felt that if she was throwing herself from a high
mountain in a deserted neighborhood nobody would
find her body and that she would just disappear from
the world. And we discussed it—that it was absolutely
necessary for her to continue treatment, and if she
wanted to commit suicide she still had time to do this
at the age of ninety-five, and then she smiled a little
bit and I said, 'We have a lot of work to do and
please let's do it together.' She seemed to be all right.
I didn't really think that she was suicidal. But she
wanted really to impress upon me how depressed she
felt at that time and she brought me the four hundred
dollars. I kept it, I think, for a week or ten days, and
then I gave it back to her and the danger passed. This
is what we call a suicidal crisis in the treatment of a
schizophrenic patient."

He was nice to her that time, she remembered. The
episode hadn't happened exactly the way he described
it—in fact, many of the details were wrong—but the
essentials were true, she had threatened to jump into

the Grand Canyon and he did keep her money for a few days to prevent her from taking the trip.

The suicide plan sounded crazy when she heard it repeated in court, but at the time it had made sense to her. It was just the idea of being found dead and helpless that was so terrifying.

Halpern was saying, "Now, doctor, we've discussed the situation between the fifteenth day of February, 1969, and August one, 1969. What was her attitude towards you? Was it one of love or one of hate, in your professional opinion?"

"She continued to hate me, although I tried to be friendly with her and encouraged her to talk to me. She said, 'I don't trust you, you are a man, I hate you.' But when I suggested she switch to a female therapist, she said she did not want to. That was a conversation that went on several times."

Julie felt outraged. It was *she* who had suggested a female therapist, and he had said that if he couldn't cure her, no one could.

Dr. Hartogs was saying that on August 4, "patient seemed to be less depressed and she talked with some relief. Now that the suicidal danger had passed, there was some kind of an opening up and she said that now she wanted to meet a former girl friend.

"She was concerned about whether the girls she had known before would still be interested in her. Whether she should contact these girls. Whether she should lift the telephone when she thought a girl friend was calling her. Because she was in the habit of not answering the phone for days in a row, just sit at home, eat pints of ice cream, drink alcohol, and play the piano."

Now she could not help laughing. Every time ice cream came up in the testimony it embarrassed her, but the way he was putting it together with alcohol and playing the piano sounded comical. The spectators must be wondering if she had a second pair of hands.

Dr. Hartogs described their sessions in August and September. Once, he said, she was "in a masochistic mood." Other times, they discussed self-improvement, but she made no real progress.

On October 12, he said, "She brought up the problem whether she could get some typing work in order to help her with her finances. I didn't say yes, and I didn't say no. But on October twenty-seventh she asked me, 'Aren't you willing to give me some work so I can make more money?' and I said to her, 'I will consider it because I have some work for you to do.' At that time I gave her a prescription for Librium, five milligrams twice a day, because she seemed to be tense."

On November 2, Dr. Hartogs said, "She was strangely excited and somewhat supercilious, semisophisticated, as usually she was when she was very hostile. At that moment I became a little bit afraid of her, because the hostility had a very strange character. She stammered that she hated me again and that the world would be much better off if all males were to be eliminated.

"At that time, I wrote a book on violence, on which I had been working for many years. I took my criteria for the predirection of violence-proneness, which permits me to predict whether a person might engage in homicide at a later date, and I found at that time that, of forty-eight criteria, she actually had thirty-two. So, this is not very dangerous, but it is an increased degree of danger where an analyst has to be careful, because some analysts have been actually killed by their paranoid patients."

On November 20, he said, "She made a statement that her life had narrow limits for survival, and she added, 'I have mostly read it in magazines.' So this was difficult to comprehend, but it was again a question of survival."

Read what in magazines? This *is* difficult to comprehend, she thought. She stole a look at the jury, hoping to catch some sign of sympathy for her, or any show of feeling. Nothing.

Dr. Hartogs was saying, "At that time I realized that I had about reached the limits I felt I could help her. It was clear that she would not improve further because one day she was improved, the other day she was again back where she came from. At that time I decided to terminate the treatment, which I discussed with her on November twenty-eighth.

"I told her that she had sufficiently improved that we would consider terminating her treatment, but she said that she wanted to maintain the contact with me and wanted to do some typing work for me, as she needed money. So that was the end of the treatment, November twenty-eighth, 1969, and from then on, this person was not a patient any more. She became very angry when sometimes she wanted to talk to me about something and I absolutely refused. She did typing and I paid her and you have the checks."

Then Halpern said, "Now, let me ask you a very direct question, doctor, and I want a truthful answer.

"Did you ever, from February fifteenth, 1969, to November twenty-eight, 1969, have sexual intercourse with this plaintiff?"

"I never engaged in sex relations with this person," Dr. Hartogs shouted.

"From the period that she became your employee after November twenty-eight, up to September of 1970, did you ever have intercourse with this plaintiff?"

"Never!"

"Did she maintain a hostility toward you from February fifteen, 1969, up to the end of September, 1970?"

"Yes, she did."

"Did that hostility ever change to affection or love?"

"It never changed. She hated me all through, up to the moment when she tried to blackmail me for a thousand dollars."

"Tell us about this thousand dollars, doctor."

He said that on October 26, 1970, "when I didn't have much work any more, she came and became very angry at me because she suspected I had engaged somebody else. She had been absent from typing for three weeks, claiming that she had broken an arm, which she admitted later on was a lie. At the moment I had to be very persistent and she said—before she slammed the door and walked out—'I am going to mess you up.' A week later this telephone call came from her asking for a thousand dollars."

"And did she say what she wanted the thousand dollars?"

"She said that she wanted to get the money back which she had paid me for her treatment, which was about six hundred and ninety or seven hundred dollars. And on the basis of my experience with paranoid schizophrenics, and as I was really afraid of her, I sent her a check for a thousand dollars, which was then returned by her attorney."

Halpern asked Dr. Hartogs to look at the photograph of the couch in his office, then asked if he had ever measured it. Dr. Hartogs said he had and that "the width is twenty-nine inches, the length is six feet." Halpern placed the photograph in evidence.

He then asked, "Now, doctor, from your many, many years of experience as a psychiatrist, can you tell me whether a person suffering from schizophrenia, paranoiac type, really believes sincerely what they say?"

"They do, absolutely."

"In other words, when this plaintiff says that she had intercourse with you, in her schizophrenic mind, does she actually believe that?"

"Yes, she does."

"Does she know the difference between reality and delusion?"

"She does not."

"Will she ever know it?"

"Never."

"Now, doctor, as far as this plaintiff is concerned, will she have this schizophrenia, the catatonic or the paranoiac type, for the rest of her life?" Halpern asked.

"Yes," said Dr. Hartogs.

"Absolutely incurable?"

"It is incurable once it has been established in early childhood, and we have reason to believe that she was disturbed very early in her childhood. She may be able to make a superficial adjustment to a job, but the basic delusional symptom will continue to exist."

After a few more questions about schizophrenia, Halpern said, "Doctor, let me ask you a very personal question. When were you married?"

"In 1936."

"And where were you married?"

"In Belgium, Antwerp."

"How long did you live together as husband and wife?"

"Until the time we divorced. That was January or February of 1970."

"Now, let me ask you this, doctor: Aside from a visible vein in your leg, and some hair above your abdomen, have you a visible imperfection on your body which is clearly visible?"

"Yes."

"What is that?"

"That's a tumor of the right testicle called a hydrocele."

"And how big is that?"

"It is five times as large as the left testicle, and it resulted from a kick of a Nazi guard—"

Cohen objected, "Your Honor, there is no—"

The judge said, "Your objection is overruled."

Dr. Hartogs went on, "It came from the kick of a Nazi guard. While I was in a concentration camp in 1940."

Halpern placed a photograph before Dr. Hartogs

and asked if it represented the condition of his testicles in 1969.

"Yes, that's what it was, and that's what it is," Dr. Hartogs said.

Halpern placed the photograph, which was in color, in evidence. Cohen asked the judge if he could conduct a "voir dire" (to speak to the point about a particular question), and the judge assented.

Cohen asked Dr. Hartogs, "Did you take this photograph, doctor?"

Dr. Hartogs said he did not and that it was taken "some years ago."

"After the litigation started?"

"Yes."

"Who took the photograph, doctor?" asked Cohen.

"A photographer sent to me by Jesse Cohen."

The judge said to Dr. Hartogs, "Now, this picture," indicating the photograph, "illustrates the condition you spoke about, the hydrocele which has been in existence from 1940 until the present time?"

"Yes," said Dr. Hartogs.

"It may be marked," said the judge, and the photograph was placed in evidence.

As the photograph was given to the jury, Julie prayed she wouldn't be asked to look at it.

Halpern asked Dr. Hartogs what year he had been divorced and Dr. Hartogs said the beginning of 1970. Halpern asked, "For many years prior to 1970 you did not have sexual intercourse with your wife?" Dr. Hartogs said not since 1965. Halpern asked the reason for this.

"It is the tumor which interfered, which is very sensitive and has to be continuously supported, and any kind of activity is painful."

"Can you participate in sexual intercourse in the condition that you are in now?" asked Halpern.

"No, absolutely not," said Dr. Hartogs.

"Could you in 1968 and 1969 and 1970 participate in sexual intercourse?"

"No."

"Doctor, there was testimony here by the plaintiff to the effect that she saw a vein on your leg and some hair on your chest. Doctor, on Sundays during the summer, where would you go after your office hours?"

"I would usually go to the beach."

"And how were you dressed?"

"I wore a sports shirt with an open collar and shorts and sandals."

"Are these the shorts and the shirt that you wore?" Halpern handed a pair of black shorts and a black fishnet shirt to Dr. Hartogs.

"Yes," he said.

"And wearing that shirt and those shorts, would your legs be visible?"

"Oh, yes."

"And would your chest be visible?"

"Yes."

Halpern asked, "Doctor, when Julie did typing for you, was there a certain procedure when she would call for the work to be done and when there was a delivery?"

"Frequently she would pick up whatever work I had, which I prepared from the beginning of the week, on

Thursdays, after her work. She typed it in the office where she worked whenever she had time. And on Sundays, she came to my office at eight o'clock in the morning and either took it along or, if I saw a few patients and could not immediately go to the beach, she would stay there and type on my typewriter."

Halpern said, "Now, doctor, one set of questions more. Was Julie ever up to your apartment?"

"Yes," he said.

"On how many occasions?"

"Once."

"Will you please tell this jury the facts and circumstances surrounding that one occasion?"

"Yes. On a Thursday night in July, '70, she happened to be in my office and she took dictation and took some work along for typing. At that time I had prepared three shopping bags full of books and magazines which I wanted to take to my apartment because my office is otherwise too cluttered. I picked them up and we were about to leave when she said, 'Could I help you?' So I said, 'Yes.' We walked towards my apartment, it is a just a few blocks, and when we arrived at the entrance door, she asked could she come up and see my apartment. I said, 'Yes, come up.'

"So we carried the magazines and the books upstairs and I gave her a short tour of the apartment. I showed her the paintings I made. I showed her the antique bed with decals on it. And after twenty minutes, I brought her down to the street. She took a taxi and went home. That was the only visit."

"Did you have intercourse with her while she was there?"

"Decidedly not."

"Doctor, did you ever take Julie to a movie?"

"Never. I had no time. I was busy from morning to night."

"What time do you usually quit at night?"

"Around ten-thirty, eleven. I start in the morning at seven o'clock."

"When was the last time you went to a movie, doctor?"

"About ten years ago."

"Doctor, did you ever take Julie to a restaurant called the Budapest?"

"I don't know of such a restaurant. I never took her."

"Doctor, if she says you took her to a movie and to a restaurant, could you explain that statement from the psychiatric point of view?"

"At that time Miss Roy was an employee, and employees frequently form some kind of feelings for a boss. Very likely she had a desire to be taken out and developed a fantasy about it. In reality, I didn't."

"And is that a concomitant part of the schizophrenia?"

"It is the delusional part of the paranoid who believes what he wishes to believe."

"In other words, when she said she went to a restaurant with you, and to a movie, she believes that to be the truth?"

"Yes."

"And she will always believe that?"

"Absolutely."

"I have no further questions," said Halpern.

"We will take a short recess," announced the judge.

After conferring with Cohen and Halpern, the judge said, "At the request of both attorneys, both of them having given me good and sufficient reason to work only half a day, we will adjourn at this time until Monday at ten o'clock." He cautioned the jury to keep an open mind and discuss the case with no one. "Have a pleasant weekend," he advised.

The taxi ride uptown was not a happy one. Dr. Hartogs' testimony had been impressive, and some of the lawyers who had been watching the trial daily told Bob, "This is the end for you." He had not minded their previous comments, which ranged from "You haven't a chance" to "You're not wearing the right clothes." But now he felt that the colored photographs of Dr. Hartogs' genitals, showing the swollen testicle, penis, and a slight stomach paunch, had been very convincing to the jury.

"Our one hope is that the examination tomorrow morning by the urologist will prove Dr. Hartogs could have sex in spite of the hydrocele," Bob said.

On Saturday morning Deborah Lans—who, at twenty-five, was the youngest associate of the law firm— went with Dr. Hartogs and one of his attorneys, Steven Bauman, to the office of a prominent New York urologist. Julie waited with Bob, Loren, and the others to hear the report on Dr. Hartogs' hydrocele.

Miss Lans finally called to announce: "Dr. Hartogs and Mr. Bauman objected to my presence at the examination, so we reached a compromise. Mr. Bauman and I sat behind a curtain in the doctor's anteroom and listened to the examination. Very little was said. Dr. Hartogs groaned a lot."

Bob spoke to the urologist, who confirmed the existence of a hydrocele in Dr. Hartogs' testicle. But, he said, he had never heard of a case of impotence caused by a hydrocele. Furthermore, the draining of a hydrocele was a ten-minute office procedure any doctor could perform; Dr. Hartogs could even perform it on himself. The tumor could also be removed by an operation.

For the first time since Dr. Hartogs mentioned the hydrocele, they felt optimistic. Now Bob could use the urologist's findings in court. But he realized that once Dr. Hartogs heard the refutation of his argument of impotence, he would change that argument. What to? Bob wondered.

On Sunday Bob's apartment again became a second headquarters as the crisis research team worked on the final stages of the trial. Bob's wife and son were away for the weekend, so the group could work without interruption. His secretary took dictation as he prepared his cross-examinations of Dr. Hartogs and Dr. Brinitzer.

On Monday morning, in the middle of a hailstorm, Nick Lewin took a taxi to Strang Clinic; he instructed the driver to wait, stumbled and fell twice as he ran in and out. Just before the trial resumed, Nick raced in, soaking wet, but triumphantly bearing photostats of Dr. Hartogs' medical records.

Bob and Loren quickly went over the records. When they looked up, there was triumph in their eyes. Bob whispered to Julie that Dr. Hartogs had been examined at the clinic in 1964, 1965, 1971, 1973, and 1974, and each time had mentioned the existence of the hydrocele. But only in 1974, on the eve of the trial, had he made a note that the hydrocele had caused him to be "impotent since 1965." Here was a chance to trap Dr. Hartogs with evidence from his own hand.

10

The cross-examination of Dr. Hartogs began on the sixth day of the trial as Cohen asked if, since 1969, Dr. Hartogs had taught in any accredited college or university. Dr. Hartogs said no.

Cohen then asked if Dr. Hartogs, since 1969, had been on the staff of any teaching hospital. Dr. Hartogs said no. He was currently on the staff of Gracie Square Hospital, a small private psychiatric hospital in New York.

Julie was impressed as she watched Bob's slow, methodical technique. First he was showing that Dr. Hartogs' long list of credentials, although impressive to a layman, lacked some important qualifications. With further questioning, Bob showed that Dr. Hartogs was not board-certified, like the expert witnesses Bob had presented. This meant he had not taken and passed two-day written and oral examinations that would entitle him to be a member of the American Board of Psychiatry and Neurology. Julie wished she had known all this before she went to see him.

Cohen asked Dr. Hartogs to take out the index cards he had used in his testimony on Friday. "Now, doctor," Cohen asked, "according to your testimony, those index cards contain writings by you that were made during the time you were treating Julie Roy, is that correct?"

"Correct."

"Did you make those entries at the end of the sessions that you had with Julie?"

"Either at the end of the session or, let's say, two or three days later. It depends on how much time I had."

"How long would you say that first session with Julie took, about a half hour?"

"No, more. The first session was about three-quarters of an hour to fifty minutes." He went on to say she had been "noncommunicative," "nonresponsive," "evasive," and "somewhat mute."

Cohen said, "Doctor, you made the following findings on this first session, am I correct? You found that she was homosexual?"

"Yes."

"You found she was divorced?"

"Yes."

"You found she was homicidal?"

Checking his notes, Dr. Hartogs said, "It says 'homicidal potential.' "

"Did you find that she was tense?"

"Tense, yes."

"Did you find that she was occasionally incoherent?"

"Occasionally, yes."

"Did you find she had occasional memory lapses?"

"Yes."

"Did you find she had a low average intelligence?"

"Yes."

"By the way, did you give her any intelligence examination that day?"

"No."

"Did you find that she was and had been depressed?"

"Yes."

"And did she tell you she disliked her job?"

"Definitely."

"And did she tell you she played the piano?"

"Yes."

"And took piano lessons?"

"Yes."

"And ate a lot of ice cream?"

"Yes."

"And drank to excess before bedtime?"

"Yes."

"And didn't answer the telephone?"

"Yes."

"And was afraid of heights?"

"That's what she said."

"And water?"

"Yes."

"And lightning?"

"Lightning."

"And thunder?"

"Yes."

For about ten minutes Cohen continued to question Dr. Hartogs on the things he claimed he had found out about Julie during their first session—her background, her feelings, her emotional state. Then Cohen said, "Doctor, the items that I have just outlined to you, consisting of both your findings and things she told you, comprise a list of over fifty items. Is it your testimony that in your first session of approximately forty-five minutes, the first portion of which consisted of meeting with the patient and introducing yourself for the first

time, she told you all of those things and you made
all of those findings? Is that your testimony?"

Dr. Hartogs said it was.

Cohen then cited an answer given by Dr. Hartogs in
his deposition, in which he said Julie had paid him a
total of $340 for her therapy but had called and in-
sisted on his giving her back $1,000. Cohen said, "She
didn't pay you three hundred and forty dollars. She
paid you seven hundred and fifteen dollars, is that correct, doctor?"

"I have six hundred and ninety," he said, consulting
a written item. "There was a second page which I
didn't see."

The judge said, "When you said three hundred and
forty dollars it was in error?"

"Error," said Dr. Hartogs.

Dr. Hartogs next said he had seen Julie on Thursdays
and Sundays before November 28, 1969, when she was
a patient, and also on Thursdays and Sundays after November 28, when she took dictation and did typing.

Cohen asked, "Now, sir, during the period that you
were treating her, you found Julie to be very sick
emotionally, did you not?"

"Yes."

"You found she was schizophrenic, is that right?"

"Yes."

"And paranoid type?"

"Correct."

"With catatonic aspects?"

"Yes."

"And you found that she retained this sickness
through your entire course of treatment, is that correct?"

"There was a mild improvement toward the end."

"As a matter of fact, at the beginning of November you made an entry that you found Julie to be very hostile, is that right?"

"She was glib and hostile in her speech and I remarked to myself that she might be homicidal."

"Sir, despite your findings in November that she was possibly homicidal, that she was violent, that she was schizophrenic, paranoid type, you found on November twenty-eight that she had sufficiently improved and you terminated treatment, is that correct, sir?"

"Yes, that's correct."

"Now, when did you first become afraid of Julie, sir?"

"Around that time."

"Did you have a real concern that she might take a gun and kill you?"

"Yes, I had."

"Despite that, sir, on November twenty-eight, you hired her to become your typist and stenographer?"

"Yes."

"Now as I understand your testimony, you didn't employ Julie as a typist until after you terminated your therapy sessions with her on November twenty-eight, is that right?"

"Yes. Let me see here." He consulted his notes. "I gave her the first check on November fifteenth."

"That was before you terminated her treatment, wasn't it, Dr. Hartogs?"

"No."

"You said you terminated her treatment on November twenty-eight, sir."

"We discussed the termination of treatment in the

last sessions, or something like that, and she started to type already while she was in treatment for one week."

Julie was pleased to see Dr. Hartogs once again caught in a trap of his own making.

"When you found you needed a secretary-typist, did you call an employment agency?" Cohen was asking.

"No, I didn't."

"One of the things she typed, sir, were letters concerning patients of yours, is that right?"

"One of the things, yes."

"Weren't you concerned, doctor, about trusting that schizophrenic, a paranoid, delusive girl, with private communications concerning your patients? Weren't you concerned that she was liable to do something violent with respect to your patients?"

"No, because her intelligence was fully maintained."

"During the period you claim she was working for you, did you recommend that she go back into therapy?"

"No, there was no reason."

"Now, as I understand your testimony, doctor, you ran out of typing work in October of 1970, is that right?"

"That's correct."

"And did you have a conversation with Julie at that time?"

"Yes. I said, 'I'm sorry. I don't have much work right now.' "

"What did she say to you, sir?"

"She became furious. She said, 'I don't believe you. You have employed somebody else and I am going to mess you up.' "

"Did she tell you how she was going to 'mess you up'?"

"No."

"Did you think that she might go into some sort of psychotic episode?"

"I was afraid of that."

"Is it fair to say that after that conversation you felt that Julie was dangerous?"

"I had some doubts in my heart, yes."

"Doubts about what, sir?"

"That Julie really could mess me up. And the fact that I am here shows me that I was right."

Cohen asked about a second conversation with Julie, the one that took place over the telephone in the early part of October, 1970.

"Julie was physically upset and demanded a thousand dollars from me," said Dr. Hartogs. "I asked her, 'What do you want a thousand dollars for?' She said, 'I want to recover monies I paid you during the treatment period of '69.' "

"Did she tell you that she was going to tell the world that you and she had sex when she was in therapy?"

"She didn't mention that, but she was very threatening."

"So that your professional opinion, as a result of those two conversations, was that Julie was likely to go into some kind of psychotic episode?"

"Not that she would break down, but that it was a reactivation of her delusional ideas."

Dr. Hartogs said he had given Julie drugs including Ovral and Ovulen, both birth-control pills, plus Prednisone and tranquilizers while she was employed by him.

The judge interrupted, saying, "Just a minute, doctor,

I would like to ask you a question that has been bothering me." He showed Dr. Hartogs Exhibit 4, a piece of paper, and asked, "Do you recognize this prescription blank of yours?"

"Yes, that's correct."

"And it's dated May nine, 1970."

"That's correct."

"That's during the employment period, right?" said the judge.

"That's right."

"Now, did you prescribe Flagyl?" asked the judge.

"Yes."

"What did you prescribe Flagyl for?" asked the judge.

"I prescribed it for treatment of alcoholism because she arrived sometimes completely drunk and she was my employee and I wanted her to function better. Flagyl tablets are used in the treatment of alcoholics, to disturb their taste of the alcohol."

The judge asked Dr. Hartogs, "Is Flagyl ever used as a specific drug for trichomoniasis vaginalis?"

"Yes, it is."

"When such a thing is prescribed for a male who is having sexual intercourse with a female, what would be the purpose of doing that?" asked the judge.

"When vaginal infections take place, then frequently there is reinfection between male and female—"

The judge interrupted, "Well, is that called a venereal infection?"

"No, not for trichomoniasis," said Dr. Hartogs.

"Is trichomoniasis vaginalis a low-grade infection?" asked the judge.

"Yes," said Dr. Hartogs.

"Can it be transmitted during intercourse?" asked the judge.

"Yes."

"And that's why both parties take it, so they shouldn't reinfect each other?"

"That's correct, yes."

"All right, you have answered my question. Thank you," said the judge.

Thank you, judge, Julie thought.

Cohen was asking Dr. Hartogs if, when he was concerned that Julie was going to "mess him up," he could have had her committed to a mental institution. Dr. Hartogs said he could not.

Then Cohen said, "You sent her a check, is that right?"

"Yes, because I was scared."

"But you didn't know what you were scared about, because she hadn't told you that she was going to claim that you had sex with her, is that right?"

"Yes."

"You were so scared that you sent her a thousand dollars within a week, is that right?"

"Yes, sir."

"Then, doctor, can you explain to me how you sent her a check for a thousand dollars in February of 1971 —four months after you claim you were so frightened?"

"I can explain it. You don't know me, but I'm not so easily scared of anybody. It takes me a long time before I really move. I have been in dangerous situations with mental patients and I have been threatened plenty, and

I have had in the last two years four holdups in my office, and I was not scared."

The judge showed Dr. Hartogs a photostat of the face of his check, marked Plaintiff's Exhibit 17, asking, "Does this refresh your recollection as to when you wrote out the check?"

"Yes," said Dr. Hartogs.

"And is the date February sixteen, 1971?" asked the judge.

"The date is correct, sir."

Cohen asked, "So, doctor, when you said you were very scared and you immediately sent her a check, you were lying, is that right?"

Halpern objected and the judge sustained his objection, but the point was made.

Cohen then asked, "Do you recall the plaintiff calling you in December of 1970, or January of 1971, and telling you that she needed her medical records for a psychiatrist that she was then in treatment with?"

"No, I don't recollect," said Dr. Hartogs.

"Do you have any recollection of her ever asking you for her medical records?"

"No."

"Doctor, isn't it a fact that you sent that check on February sixteen, 1971, to Julie after she asked you for her medical records and you told her not to tell her new psychiatrist that you and she had sex together?"

"That is not so."

"Do you ascribe to the American Psychiatric Association's canon insofar as patients having sex with their psychiatrists [is concerned]?"

"Yes."

"Is it your professional opinion that patients should not have sex with their psychiatrists?"

"Yes."

"Have you ascribed to that since 1948, when you were a psychiatric resident in Canada?"

"Yes."

"Since 1948 and up till the present time, have you ever had sex with any of your patients?"

"No."

"And you never had sex with Julie Roy either, did you, doctor?"

"No."

"Have you ever suggested that any of your patients have sex with you, doctor?"

"No."

"Have you ever, since 1948, fondled any of your patients in a sexual manner?"

"No."

"Now, doctor, as I understand your testimony, starting in 1965, you were unable to have an erection, is that your testimony?"

"No."

"Have you been able to have an erection since 1965?"

"Yes."

"Is it your testimony, then, that since 1965 it became too painful to have sex with anybody?"

"Yes."

"And so it is not, doctor, that you are impotent, but that you have too much pain to have sex, is that right?"

"Correct."

"When did you discover for the first time that there was too much pain?"

"It started in '64."

"Did you have sex in 1964 with anybody?"

"I imagine with my wife, but it was very painful."

"Did you have sex in 1965, doctor?"

"No, we stopped."

"Doctor, did you have a fairly robust sexual life prior to 1964?"

"Robust, what's that?"

"You are a psychiatrist, you hear about people's sex lives all the time. Did you think your sex life was fairly active?"

"It was normal, but it petered out."

The spectators roared at this unconscious pun.

The judge asked, "At the time it was normal, did you enjoy sex?"

"As long as it didn't hurt, I enjoyed it."

Julie almost cheered as she heard Bob getting Dr. Hartogs to admit that he had not been impotent after all, only that it was "painful" to have sex. Of course, only he could measure his "pain," thus making him immune to any expert witness's testimony.

Cohen questioned Dr. Hartogs about his hydrocele. Dr. Hartogs said he went to Europe and saw two physicians who advised against an operation because the hydrocele would only return. He said he had gone to the Strang Clinic only to make sure the hydrocele was not cancerous. He said he also once consulted a surgeon, who was currently "out of town."

Through questioning, Cohen brought out the fact that over a period of ten years when Dr. Hartogs visited the Strang Clinic he said nothing about impotence, but in 1974, he wrote on the form "right testicle often painful, impotence since 1965."

Cohen also noted that under "chief health problems" Dr. Hartogs had listed "diarrhea" and "hemorrhoids." Cohen asked, "Did you, anyplace on that list, state that you couldn't have sexual intercourse, as a chief health problem?"

"It is not a chief health problem," replied Dr. Hartogs. "My health is not endangered by impotence, or whatever it is."

"And according to your testimony, doctor, this hydrocele condition developed in the early 1940s, is that correct?"

"In 1940."

"Approximately when did it get to its present size, according to you?"

"I would say in '64."

"Was it visible to anybody having sex with you in 1945?"

"Yes."

Cohen asked if a hydrocele was fairly common among men, especially in their fifties and sixties, and Dr. Hartogs said yes. Cohen asked if Dr. Hartogs was aware of a simple procedure called a draining that could reduce the hydrocele so the scrotum appeared normal, and Dr. Hartogs said yes, adding, "I am not only aware but I had it and it didn't do any good."

Cohen asked, "Are you aware that the procedure is so simple that you could even perform it upon yourself?"

"I wouldn't dare."

"The draining procedure would not leave any mark on your scrotum, would it?"

"No."

"So that if you had a draining done, there would be no way to tell that it had been done, is that correct?"

"That's correct."

Then followed Halpern's redirect examination. He asked Dr. Hartogs if, at any time, he had taken Flagyl. Dr. Hartogs said no.

Only too true, Julie thought, remembering the months of discomfort and fear when she couldn't get rid of the trichomoniasis. That, and a box of candy with several pieces missing, were the only things Dr. Hartogs ever gave her.

Halpern showed Dr. Hartogs a letter he had written to Dr. Sencer reporting his treatment of Julie. Dr. Hartogs affirmed he had sent it. Then, in recross-examination, Cohen asked Dr. Hartogs if he had been in error when he testified that Julie Roy had never asked him to send her medical records anyplace and Dr. Hartogs said yes, he had forgotten about the report to Dr. Sencer.

Referring to the notes Dr. Hartogs claimed he made while Julie was under his care, Cohen asked if Dr. Hartogs had checked the cards when he wrote Dr. Sencer. Dr. Hartogs said no, he had relied on his memory.

Cohen said, "Isn't it a fact, sir, that these cards never existed in 1968 and '69 and '70, so that you couldn't refer to them, and that you prepared them for trial?"

"No, certainly not," said Dr. Hartogs.

"Doctor, you told Dr. Sencer that Julie was in treatment for 1968 and 1969, do you recall that?"

"Is it in the letter?"

"I will show you the letter. Did you tell Dr. Sencer Julie was in treatment with you for two years, '68 and '69?"

"I was in error," Dr. Hartogs said.

Cohen asked, "You testified in ten years you didn't have time to go to the movies. How did you have time to go to the beach?"

"Because the beach was very important to me. Movies are totally uninteresting, and I don't spend my only free time to go to them."

"So when you said, doctor, that you didn't have time to go to the movies, what you meant is you didn't have an interest in going to the movies?"

The judge declared a luncheon recess.

It was another working lunch for Bob, Loren, and Julie. This noon, she noticed, there were television and newspaper reporters who wanted to talk to Bob. He told them he was not permitted to make any statements to the press during the trial.

She knew Bob had done a fine job in proving Dr. Hartogs inaccurate on so many points, and yet the hydrocele was still a haunting issue. The verdict might depend largely on the extent to which the jury was convinced by the spectacular colored photograph. She hoped it would occur to them that a hydrocele drained any number of times and then permitted to grow to an impressive size if a man wished.

11

Dr. Hartogs' lone psychiatric witness, Dr. Walter Brinitzer, was called to the stand to open the afternoon session. Julie remembered her one-hour interview with him the previous year. He had seemed sympathetic, even though he was in Dr. Hartogs' camp. He spoke with a German accent and his facial features were rather sharp, she thought.

Dr. Brinitzer told the court he obtained his medical degree in 1935 in Germany, arrived in New York in 1949, became a United States citizen and got his New York State medical license that year. He had worked full time at Creedmore Hospital in Queens for seventeen years as a supervising psychiatrist and had been a consultant at Long Island Jewish Hospital and Hillside Hospital. For the past six years he had been director of the psychiatric services of Mary Immaculate Hospital, a part of the Catholic Medical Center. He was also consultant to two methadone units handling five hundred patients, and was in private practice.

He said he had examined Julie Roy in his office at the request of Dr. Hartogs' lawyer on March 22, 1973. She had been accompanied by Loren Plotkin. He described Julie Roy as "a very frightened, fragile person. She shied away from a most miniature poodle that came to greet her on entry into the apartment. She kept her winter coat on for the duration of the interview, though the office was well heated. The way she insisted on it was interpreted by me as an insecure feeling."

He continued, "She settled down and soon seemed to feel at ease. She was cooperative, was controlled, tried and even managed to be pleasant. As she became more relaxed, her answering style changed from words to sentences and from short ones to longer ones. However, she found it difficult, so she said, to express herself spontaneously and in continuity other than in response to questions. She spoke in a soft voice, free from anger and hostility. Her feeling tone was neither happy nor depressed. In fact, her emotional reactions were remarkably dull, constricted, flat, and blunted."

He described her childhood, her social and scholastic failures, her weight problem.

"The pattern of isolation, immaturity, and dependence on food has continued to be with her up to the present day," he said. "She has an often occurring nightmare of 'people watching me.' She denies delusions of persecution and of being watched when awake and claims to know the difference between fact and fantasy, between reality and imagination at all times. No hallucinations were observed or elicited."

He described her as "very unsure of her feelings in general." He said a few psychological test questions "reveal a typical schizophrenic way of thinking concretely and show her inability to abstract."

Dr. Brinitzer concluded that in his opinion, her condition could best be described as "catatonic schizophrenia." He predicted she would suffer from this condition the rest of her life, and that it would get "worse and worse as it goes along." He claimed she could not differentiate between reality and delusion. In maintaining she had sexual relations with Dr. Hartogs, he said, "she is suffering from delusions instead of fact."

He quoted from "an excellent report at hand by Dr. Anderson," saying, "It comes out with findings that agreed with mine, or I agree with hers." He said he did not believe Julie Roy's condition was "worsened" by the treatment she had received from Dr. Hartogs.

In cross-examination, Cohen asked Dr. Brinitzer what fee he was getting, and he said $1,000. Cohen also asked if Dr. Brinitzer relied "heavily" on Dr. Anderson's report.

"Yes," he said, "I found her report most revealing. I consider her a well-qualified person."

"Are you aware, doctor, that Dr. Anderson testified in this court that in her professional opinion Julie was not deluded, and Julie did have sex with Dr. Hartogs?"

"I am not aware of that fact at all," said Dr. Brinitzer.

"If you knew that Dr. Anderson, after spending eight months with Julie, found that Julie was telling the truth insofar as her sexual relationship with Dr. Hartogs [was concerned], would that change your professional opinion?"

"Yes," said Dr. Brinitzer.

Cohen asked Dr. Brinitzer, "Would it be a disaster for a psychiatrist to have sex in psychotherapy with a schizophrenic, doctor?"

Halpern objected to the form of the question, so Cohen rephrased it. "Would it seriously adversely affect a schizophrenic patient if her psychiatrist had sex with her?"

"No," said Dr. Brinitzer.

"It would have no effect on her?"

"No."

"How would it affect her, doctor?" Cohen tried again.

"In that the therapist cannot give his best," said Dr. Brinitzer.

Cohen asked Dr. Brinitzer if he was certified by the American Board of Psychiatry and Neurology and Dr. Brinitzer said no. He also said he was not teaching at any accredited college or university.

Bob's brother-in-law, Dr. Alan Tuckman, who had helped on the case, was in court that day and sitting next to Julie in the front row. She was delighted to have his company, and noticed that he seemed as stunned as she when Dr. Brinitzer testified that a psychiatrist's engaging in sex with a schizophrenic patient would have no ill effect on the patient but would interfere with the doctor's giving his "best."

At one point Alan and she laughed over a sketch a television artist was drawing of Dr. Hartogs; no cameras were allowed in court. She asked Alan whom he thought the sketch looked like and he said it was a perfect image of Freud, that the artist's subjectivity was showing. If she could draw her own sketch of Dr. Hartogs, she thought, he would come out looking like Rasputin, with strange, messianic eyes.

She envied Alan's patients. They must love him very much, she thought, but then she was fortunate in her own way. She'd managed to pick a pretty bad psychiatrist, but look at her attorneys! On the other hand, she realized, with a psychiatrist like Alan, patients wouldn't need any attorneys.

The last witness for the defendant was called: Dr. Hartogs' ex-wife, Mrs. Nelly Hartogs. Necks craned among the spectators as the attractive woman, dark glasses hiding her eyes, took the stand.

Asked for her background, Mrs. Hartogs said, "I have a Ph.D. in sociology which I got in '65, and in '44 I got a degree in social work at Columbia University. Until 1960 I worked as a social worker and in 1960 I decided to go back to school. Since 1965, when I got my degree, I have been doing research in social welfare problems." She said she married Dr. Hartogs in 1936.

"You are divorced now, aren't you?" Halpern asked.

"Yes," she said.

"When were you divorced?"

"In January, 1970."

Julie felt sorry for this woman; she must be dying of shame. Julie remembered a time she called Dr. Hartogs from a phone booth and in looking up his number saw a Dr. Nelly Hartogs listed at the same address. She asked him if that was his wife. He said, "Former wife." What kind of doctor was she? A sociologist, he said. And that was as much as she knew about Mrs. Hartogs, until now.

Mrs. Hartogs was saying she had lived with Dr. Hartogs in the same premises until 1970 and that sexual relations between them had ceased "around the '64–'65 period."

"Can you give this jury a reason for the cessation of sexual relations between your husband and yourself?" asked Halpern.

"It was a combination of two things. He had trouble —physical troubles—that had increased over the years, and we'd also grown apart."

"And since 1964 or '65, up to the date of your divorce, you had no contact with him in the form of sexual relationship?"

"Definitely not."

In his cross-examination, Cohen asked, "Dr. Hartogs, you have no idea whether since 1965 your husband had sex with anybody else, do you?"

"Objected to," said Halpern, and the judge sustained the objection.

"Did you live with Dr. Hartogs continuously until 1970, doctor?" Cohen asked.

"Yes."

"And were there periods of time when you were separated from him between 1965 and 1970?"

"You will have to explain 'separated.' "

"For example, did you know that Dr. Hartogs went on a convention to Japan?"

"Yes."

"And you didn't go with him on that convention, did you?"

"No."

"Did you know that he took another woman with him on that convention?"

"No."

The judge said, "The jury is cautioned that the fact that the question was asked doesn't constitute any evidence that the doctor took another woman to Japan with him. The answer to that question was 'No.' "

"Did Dr. Hartogs take any trips other than that 1969 trip, between '65 and '69?" asked Cohen.

"Objected to as irrelevant," said Halpern, and was sustained.

Cohen objected, "Your Honor, I think I am entitled

to show that there were substantial periods of time when she wasn't with him and she couldn't possibly know what his sex life was."

The judge replied, "I don't think you can learn from her what his relationships were with anybody else, if there were any."

Cohen asked a few questions about the Hartogs' divorce, then said, "Mrs. Hartogs, was that divorce precipitated by the fact that you learned that Dr. Hartogs was having sex with patients?"

Halpern objected and was sustained.

Cohen asked, "Did you receive any payments from Dr. Hartogs when you separated?"

"Objected to," said Halpern.

Cohen explained he wanted to "show bias" on the part of the witness, because Mrs. Hartogs' alimony or other income or property might suffer if her ex-husband lost the verdict. The judge ruled against this.

After Mrs. Hartogs was excused, it was time for the plaintiff's rebuttal. Now the judge would allow Cohen to call in several "female witnesses," as he had requested.

There was a stir of excitement in the courtroom. Word had spread that the case was about to burst wide open.

12

~~~~~~

A slim, light-haired woman in her forties nervously stepped up to the witness stand. She told the court her name was Mrs. Pauline David. She lived in New Jersey, and had taught for twenty years in the New York school system.

Cohen asked, "Mrs. David, were you ever a patient of Dr. Renatus Hartogs?"

"Yes, I was," she said.

"And when did you first commence being a patient with Dr. Hartogs?"

"In October, 1965."

"For how long, starting with 1965, did you see Dr. Hartogs as a psychiatrist?"

"I saw him beginning in October, 1965, three times a week, Monday, Wednesday, and Friday, until October, 1972."

She said she paid $10 a visit.

"Did there come a time, after you began treatment with Dr. Hartogs, when you and he had sex together in his office?" Cohen asked.

"Yes," she said.

"When did that occur for the first time?"

"Approximately the second week."

"Did it continue during the course of your treatment?"

"Yes, it did regularly."

"Until you terminated treatment in 1972?"

"That's right."

"How often did you have sex with Dr. Hartogs?"

"About once a week."

"Where did that take place?"

"Always in his office."

"At any point during the period of time that you were having sexual intercourse with him, did he ever complain to you that he had too much pain?"

"Never," she said.

"Did you see Dr. Hartogs nude from time to time in his office?"

"Yes, every week."

"Did you notice anything wrong with his testicles or his penis?"

"Absolutely not."

"Now, approximately how long were the sessions that you had with Dr. Hartogs?"

"They were never more than half an hour, but they were occasionally less, like ten minutes, fifteen minutes."

"When you had sex with Dr. Hartogs in his office, where did you have sex with him?"

"On the couch."

"I am going to show you Defendant's Exhibit One in evidence and ask you whether that's the couch where you and Dr. Hartogs had sex." He handed her the photograph.

"Yes," she said.

"Mrs. David, did you continue to pay Dr. Hartogs for each session that you had, including the sessions that you had sex with him?"

"Absolutely."

Under cross-examination by Halpern, Mrs. David said

she had been married twelve years and had three children, and that she was separated for nine years before she got a divorce.

Halpern said, "You don't like Hartogs, do you?"

"No," said Mrs. David.

"And during the seven years, you willingly had intercourse with him?"

"Yes."

"You came to his office three times a week?"

"That's right."

"Did you go there knowing that you were going to have intercourse with him?"

"I am sorry, sir, I don't understand what you mean," said Mrs. David. "I was very passive about it. If Dr. Hartogs wished to have intercourse, then we did. I never instigated any session of intercourse."

"And was that during a period that you were married?"

"I was legally separated, but not divorced."

"What did you go to Dr. Hartogs for treatment for?"

"I had some tragic experiences. My parents died the same day. My father committed suicide when he heard of my mother's death. A month after that, my son had a brain injury, lost his eyesight temporarily. I was obliged to support my three children during this period. I found I was very tense. One day by chance I met a patient of Dr. Hartogs' and she recommended that I go to him."

"Did you continue to be upset for a period of seven years?"

"No, in the beginning, I was very optimistic—the first year and a half. As time went on during the treatment, instead of feeling better, I seemed to be lethargic, depressed, not doing my work as well as I should. At least I felt that way, and this seemed to get progressively worse."

"And you still continued to go to him?"

"Dr. Hartogs assured me that I was not in a position to tell whether I was getting better or not, but that he was certain I was improving."

"How did the treatments terminate?"

"I was extremely upset the last two weeks. I was unable to sleep. I was getting very, very tense and depressed and uncomfortable. I was having nightmares and I felt that I just couldn't kid myself any longer. I couldn't believe Dr. Hartogs. I wanted to go to another doctor. I simply felt I must get away from this setup. He implored me not to stop. I cut out treatment."

Halpern asked if she raised any objections to the sex during her treatment and she said, "I tried on numerous occasions to stop and he kept saying, 'Trust me' and 'You need this love. You have been deprived.' "

Halpern made what is called an offer of proof outside the hearing of the jury. He told the judge, "The court is permitting another case to be tried in this case." The judge said, "This proof has been admitted for one purpose and one purpose only. The defendant testified that for the last ten years, because of a physical ailment, he had no sexual intercourse. This lady now says that during this ten-year period she had sexual intercourse with him."

Halpern said, "I move for a mistrial on the ground that her testimony is highly prejudicial and the rulings are highly prejudicial."

"Your motion is denied," said Judge Myers.

Halpern continued his cross-examination, asking Mrs.

David if she had ever observed Dr. Hartogs' "sexual organs."

"Not carefully, merely casually as he walked," she said.

"Did you see anything wrong, anything out of the ordinary?"

"Absolutely not."

Halpern asked about her reasons for agreeing to testify. Mrs. David said at first she had refused, knowing her name would appear in newspaper accounts. But she changed her mind, she said, because she knew that otherwise "my conscience would embarrass me."

There were tears in Julie's eyes as she listened to Mrs. David's story, and she could hear other people sniffling into their handkerchiefs. She stood up to hug Mrs. David as she left the court, thanked her for coming. She half expected the judge or Mr. Halpern to object, but no one said a word.

The next witness was Judith Ann Cuttler. She said she learned of the trial through the *New York Post,* and explained that she had written to Julie and her lawyers with the help of Sheila Moran.

She said she was a senior at Cooper Union, where she was studying filmmaking. She also taught a drawing class for disadvantaged high school students and was a secretary-typist at the United Cerebral Palsy Foundation.

She testified she had become a patient of Dr. Hartogs toward the end of January, 1969, and had continued seeing him, except for a month-and-a-half interruption when she was unemployed, until the first week of October, 1970.

She said she had paid Dr. Hartogs $10 for one session a week until the fall of 1969, when her parents contributed $20 a week so she could see him three times weekly. Cohen asked how long her sessions were and she said, "They became shorter and shorter." Dr. Hartogs had originally agreed to a half-hour session, she said, but by the time she stopped seeing him, "many of them were only ten minutes long."

Cohen asked, "Now, during any of the period that you saw Dr. Hartogs, did he ever fondle your breasts?"

"Yes," she said.

"And could you tell us how that occurred and how he did that?"

"It began to happen about three to six months after I had been seeing him. He began to make the end of the session sort of like a goodbye kiss. He would stand at the doorway and say things to me like 'Give me a little kiss, darling.' And then he would start to touch me, and it is difficult to describe it because I was very uncomfortable. Sometimes he would reach under my blouse. I didn't wear a bra so he touched my breast. He would do other things too, always initiated by him."

"Did he ever put his hands inside your pants?"

"Yes, at least once."

"Did he ever press his penis up against your body?"

"Yes. I can remember clearly at least two times."

"Did he ever complain there was any pain to him when he did that?"

"No, never," she said.

In cross-examination, Halpern asked, "Judy, did you ever have sexual intercourse with him?"

"No," she said.

"Did he ever suggest that you have sexual intercourse with him?"

"I think you could say he did," she answered. "Because once in the middle of a session he asked me—I am trying to remember the exact words. Something like 'Would you like me to screw you?' or 'Do you want me to fuck you?' I thought about it and I said, 'No.' He said, 'Why not?' I explained to him that it would be like incest for me because I saw him like my father."

Halpern asked, "Did you ever complain to your mother or father, who were paying part of the bills, that he was fondling your breasts?"

"No," she said. "I really couldn't tell them."

"Why did you go to Dr. Hartogs, what was wrong with you?" asked Halpern.

She said some friends had commented that she seemed very nervous, and suggested she undergo an examination to show whether she needed therapy. She went to the Community Guidance Service, saw Dr. Hartogs for a consultation, and, she recalled, "He said, 'Yes, you need treatment, and I will be the person that you will see.'"

The judge called a recess.

She noticed the room was buzzing under the impact of the day's testimony. Bob told her that among the spectators were several women who told him they too had had sexual experiences with their psychotherapists, and their rage seemed to spread through the courtroom.

As the court reconvened, the judge said, "I want absolute quiet in the courtroom. If I hear any whispering, you will go out."

Then he announced, "Members of the jury, the testimony of the last witness is completely stricken from the record. You are not to consider it at all. It is not to enter into your determinations whatsoever. I am going to ask each one of you whether or not you can do that."

He polled the jurors and each one replied, "Yes." The judge warned, "It is as if you never heard it. That's on the court's own motion."

Then he asked Cohen, "Do you have any other witnesses?"

"Yes, I do, judge," Cohen said.

"If they are witnesses of this nature, don't offer them," said the judge. "You better give me an offer of proof before you put your next witness on the stand. I don't want a repetition of what just happened."

The judge declared another short recess, during which he told Cohen outside the hearing of the jury, "Just so the record will be clear. With reference to the testimony of Judith Ann Cuttler, I want to state that it is inflammatory. Its prejudicial effect so outweighed any minimal impeachment value that it might have that it never should have been placed before the jury. I think it was a terrible thing for counsel to have done." He said it did not involve sexual intercourse, which was the issue at stake.

Cohen explained why he had presented Miss Cuttler. "Your Honor, Dr. Hartogs has denied each point that Cuttler testified to—that he fondled patients, that he pressed his penis against patients, and that he suggested sex to patients. She was brought in for the purpose of impeaching his credibility in all of those areas."

"That is not the main issue in the case," said the judge, "and therefore it should not have been offered."

Halpern said, "I just want to go on record in asking for a mistrial at this point."

"Since I polled the jury and told them to disregard it, and struck the testimony from the record, I am denying your motion," said the judge.

"Thank you," said Halpern in irony.

The judge ordered the trial to proceed. Cohen called to the stand his final witness, Madeleine Thornton-Sherwood.

She said she was an actor, teacher, director, and counselor. She had performed in twenty Broadway plays, ten movies, and hundreds of television shows, including a four-year run as Mother Superior in *The Flying Nun,* and had directed a play in 1974 at the Circle in the Square, where she taught acting. She also taught at New York University and Pace University, and ran a Woman in the Arts group.

Ms. Thornton-Sherwood testified she had been a patient of Dr. Hartogs in 1949, when she lived in Montreal.

"I was very disturbed during those years," she said. "I was married. I had had a background of suicide attempts and—and—pardon me—" She started to cry.

After composing herself, she went on, "I was married and I had a child, about three. For some time I had wished to see a psychiatrist because I knew that I was disturbed about my relationship with my daughter."

She said she had gone to the Royal Victoria Hospital and had seen Dr. Hartogs at the clinic for a few visits, and "then he suggested that I see him privately in his private practice," which she did for three months.

Cohen asked, "Did you have sexual intercourse with—"

Halpern said, "I am going to object to this."

"Yes, I did," she answered.

The judge asked, "Madam, when did you terminate treatment with Dr. Hartogs?"

"When he refused to see me any longer."

"When was that?" asked the judge.

"At the beginning of 1949," she said.

"The objection is sustained. It is too remote," said the judge.

"It is not remote to me, sir," said Ms. Thornton-Sherwood.

The judge asked the court officer to escort her from the stand. As she walked past the first row of the spectators' section, she leaned over and embraced Julie.

Judge Myers reprimanded Cohen for introducing Ms. Thornton-Sherwood's testimony. Cohen maintained it was important to refute the claim of Dr. Hartogs that as a psychiatric resident he never performed a sexual act with a patient.

"It is a collateral issue," said the judge.

Cohen said, "Your Honor, I am going to make an offer of proof in connection with my next witness. She had sex with Dr. Hartogs from the period of 1957 to 1962 while in therapy at his office in New York, and I ask that the court permit me to go into that evidence with that witness."

"All right, that's closer," said the judge. "I will allow it."

"Your Honor, that witness will not be here until two o'clock." It was not yet noon.

"No, I will not allow it," said the judge. "I believe that we have now run out of time, and that since this is merely cumulative testimony, and is not essential to the plaintiff, I shall exercise my discretion to expedite the trial."

Halpern now called Dr. Hartogs to the stand. "Doctor, were you in court when Pauline David testified?" he asked.

"Yes, I was."

"Did you hear her testimony?"

"Yes."

"Now, let me ask you this. Did you ever have sexual intercourse with Pauline David?"

"Never."

"Doctor, what was your diagnosis of her mental condition?"

"She was a paranoid personality."

"And was she paranoiac throughout the entire time that you treated her?"

"Yes."

In cross-examination, Cohen asked, "Doctor, is it your testimony that Pauline David has a delusion with respect to whether she was having sex with you or not?"

"Yes."

Cohen asked, "Doctor, does she carry this delusion, according to you, while she is teaching in the public school system in the state of New York?"

"A delusion of her kind, erotomania, is monosymptomatic, which means that the individual can be nondelusional, for instance, in areas of school or work, but that in one area, and that is the area of sex or love, the individual has the delusions. These are called monosymptomatic delusions and they cannot be cured."

All the arguments were over, and both sides rested their cases. The judge dismissed the jury until two o'clock, when, he said, the attorneys would present their summations and he his charge.

Then Halpern made a motion to dismiss the case, saying the plaintiff had failed to show evidence of malpractice. He also said there had been no proof to back up the other charges in the bill of particulars, "because there was not one word here indicating any rape."

The judge said, "Both the defendant himself and every other expert that testified stated that for a psychiatrist, prescribing sex as therapy is malpractice." He said that if the jury believed Julie Roy's testimony, "the court must find that it is malpractice." He rejected Halpern's motion to dismiss the case.

The judge then suggested to both counsel that perhaps only one issue ought to go to the jury, that of malpractice, eliminating the charges of seduction and violation of the New York State penal code.

With the help of the crisis research team, Bob and Loren weighed the judge's suggestion during the lunch recess. If they agreed to drop some of the charges, would the jury think they were giving in to Dr. Hartogs, thus admitting a weakness in their case?

This was Julie's first chance to ask Bob how he knew Dr. Hartogs had taken a woman to Japan while his wife stayed home. Bob told her he had found this out from a psychiatrist friend who had been on the same trip.

She and Bob ate nothing. To her delight she had lost eight pounds since the trial began. Bob lost ten, and Loren five.

They all sensed Pauline David had made a stunning impact on the jury, whose faces nevertheless retained that impassive look they had shown from the start. But the spectators' reaction left no doubt of the force of her testimony. Gasps of indignation, startled expressions, and tears attested to a mounting sympathy for Julie.

As the trial resumed, Judge Myers asked if Cohen would agree to withdraw all the claims except the one on malpractice. Cohen, in accordance with his colleagues' advice, said he would. But he asked the judge not to inform the jury the plaintiff had withdrawn portions of the complaint. This, Cohen explained, would avoid a psychological feeling on the part of the jury that the plaintiff had backed down. The judge consented.

Then the attorneys gave their summations.

Julie listened impassively as Halpern recapped his arguments. By now she was so accustomed to his technique that she didn't flinch as he asked the jurors if they could possibly take the word of this "diseased person" against that of a respected psychiatrist.

Then Bob stood up for his summation, and again she was grateful for the clear way he presented her story. He contrasted the consistency of her testimony with the weaknesses in Dr. Hartogs' ever shifting defense, and concluded, "The Julies of the world, the sick and the wounded, need our protection more than anybody else.

For the Julies of the world, I ask you to bring in a verdict for the plaintiff."

The judge called a five-minute recess. Then he charged the jury, helping define the issues of the case.

"The issue which you have the responsibility of defendant are psychotic delusion or fact," he said. "Fact ciding is whether the plaintiff's charges against the deor fantasy."

He warned, "Keep in mind that you are not here to pass judgment on the morals of the litigants but just to decide the narrow issues of this case."

He explained he was submitting the case in two parts, saying, "I am going to ask you to answer to the following question: Did the defendant, Dr. Hartogs, a psychiatrist, induce the plaintiff, Julie Roy, to have sexual intercourse with him while she was his patient, and did he, in fact, have such intercourse with her?"

He explained that if the jurors answered this question in the negative, their answer would dispose of the entire case. If they answered in the affirmative, he said, the jury would again be asked to render a verdict, this time on the question of damages.

"You may now retire for your deliberations," the judge told the jury.

It was 3:40 P.M., Tuesday, March 18, 1975.

It seemed an army surged into the halls to wait out the verdict. The only place to sit was on the deep ledges that covered the air-conditioning and heating units, and Loren and Julie perched atop one, talking for a while to Sheila Moran and Judy Coburn, a free-lance writer. Bob was too nervous to speak to anyone. A trial was in progress down the hall and he decided to sit in, saying it would take his mind off the wait. He told Julie, "If we have to wait more than half an hour, we've lost. This should be a fast verdict if we win, because the jury either believes your story or doesn't believe it. If they believe Hartogs' story, they'll have to wrestle it out."

It was more than two hours before the jury announced it had reached a decision.

13

Julie took her usual place in the front row. Dr. Hartogs abandoned his customary seat at the opposite end to join his attorneys at the counsel table. He took the chair vacated by Loren, who now sat beside her. Loren had told Bob, "I want to be with Julie in case the verdict is negative."

A hush fell on the crowded courtroom. Though it was six o'clock, no one seemed to have left. Law clerks, lawyers, witnesses, and spectators sat or stood, shoulder to shoulder, awaiting her particular moment of truth.

The judge said, "Call in the jury."

The jury filed in.

The judge asked the forewoman, "Have you arrived at a verdict?"

"We have, Your Honor," she said.

"Will you hand the verdict up to me?" said the judge.

She gave a slip of paper to the court officer, who passed it to Judge Myers. On it were six signatures in answer to the question the judge had posed, with a place for each juror to write "Yes" or "No."

The judge read aloud. "The question: Did the defendant, Dr. Hartogs, a psychiatrist, induce the plaintiff, Julie Roy, to have sexual intercourse with him while she was his patient, and did he, in fact, have such intercourse with her?"

*   *   *

Julie took a deep breath.

The judge said to the forewoman, "Five out of the six members of this jury answered the question, 'Yes,' is that correct?"

"Yes," she said.

There was a collective gasp, then an outburst. Some women were crying, some shrieked with joy; everyone seemed to have an intense reaction. Bob jumped up from the counsel table, tears in his eyes, and started toward Julie.

Julie asked Loren, "We lost?" He put his arm around her and said, "No, we won! We won!"

She looked at Dr. Hartogs' face; it was blank. She felt stunned by the victory.

Judge Myers banged his gavel. "Will everybody please be seated."

When the courtroom was again quiet, the judge polled the jury, asking each member in turn, "Was that your verdict?" The forewoman was the lone dissenting juror.

The judge informed the jurors that the next morning they would hear the question of damages, the second phase of the summations, and his charge. Then he declared a recess until ten o'clock the following day.

Dr. Hartogs left the courtroom quickly. Several women rushed up to Bob, congratulated him, thanked him. Madeleine Thornton-Sherwood hugged Julie, saying, "This is a victory for all women."

Outside the courtroom photographers rushed at Julie,

snapped her picture, along with Bob and Loren. The trial was not over yet, so they could not answer reporters' questions. They broke away from the crowd and taxied uptown, still unable to relax, for there was work to be done on the question of damages. They stayed in the office until around nine, then went out for a modest dinner celebration. They hoped they would have more cause for celebration the following night.

On her way to court the next morning, people stopped her on the street to congratulate her. Some recognized her from television reports the night before, others from her photograph on the front page of the *Daily News*. Her case had captured the popular imagination as well as the attention of psychiatrists and lawyers.

Now, on the seventh and final day of the trial, the jury was to decide the amount of damages. She recalled Bob's saying to her when she asked how he had arrived at the figure of $1,250,000, "How do you put a price on someone's psychic integrity?"

Halpern again gave his summation first. Asking, "Where is the damage to this woman? What has she suffered?" he charged that Julie Roy "had, to begin with, a paranoia that she had throughout the case, and when she finished." He asserted that Julie, because of "her own filthy indiscretions," was not entitled to "even five cents," and pleaded with the jury to return a verdict to that effect.

In his summation Cohen described Julie as going to Dr. Hartogs for treatment of "an emotional cancer" and said Dr. Hartogs had "dispensed the wrong medicine" to "satisfy his own greed, his own lust." Cohen referred to her two hospitalizations, asking, "What price can you put on a day in a psychiatric ward?"

Declaring that Julie now had "a heavy, heavy toll that she must carry with her for the rest of her life," he asked the jury to come out with a verdict for compensatory damages in the amount of $250,000.

On the question of punitive damages, to punish Dr. Hartogs for what he had done, and "to set an example for every other professional," he asked an award of $1,000,000.

Judge Myers, in his charge to the jury, told them they must now decide whether Julie's condition had been "worsened or aggravated by reason of the defendant's malpractice and, if so, to what extent."

The jury left the courtroom at 12:30 P.M. to begin deliberations.

For the first time, Julie and Bob joined Loren for lunch outside the courtroom. She realized Bob felt free to eat because there were no more sessions to prepare for. Still, this was another time of tension. So much was at stake, she thought, not only for herself but for her attorneys.

At 2:08 the jury returned with its verdict.

The judge said, "Will you please rise, Madam Foreman? Have you arrived at a verdict?"

"We have, Your Honor," said the forewoman. "Our verdict is, Part One, compensatory, two hundred and fifty thousand dollars. Part Two, punitive, one hundred thousand dollars."

"Is that unanimous?" asked the judge.

"No, sir. Part One, the vote is six to zero. Part Two, punitive, the vote is five to one."

"All right, you may be seated," said the judge.

He polled the jury to verify the verdict, and again the one dissenting vote was the forewoman's. Then the judge said, "The jury will step outside for a few moments while I entertain motions."

After they left, Halpern moved "to set aside the verdict on the compensatory damages as abnormally excessive," and to set aside the punitive verdict as "contrary to fact, excessive, and exorbitant."

Cohen argued, "I think that the jury's award is perfectly consistent with the evidence in this case."

The judge gave both parties one week to submit memoranda on the question. Then he asked the jury to return. He thanked each member for giving the case "the careful thought and deliberation which you did," adding, "I hope you derived some sense of satisfaction out of acting as a jury and being part of the judicial process."

He discharged the jury and announced, "The court is now in recess."

Inside the courtroom Julie was again besieged by well-wishers; outside, press and cameramen surrounded her. She told Bob she did not wish to be interviewed at that moment, and Bob invited the reporters to his office at four o'clock.

Riding back in the taxi for the last time, Bob, Loren, and Julie mused over the paradoxical behavior of the forewoman, who had voted $250,000 in compensatory damages after not believing Julie's story, as recorded in her earlier vote, then voted against punitive damages.

She asked Bob to help her prepare something to say to the press. He advised, "Just tell them how you feel."

She felt heady as cameras focused on her, lights blinded her, and reporters fired questions. She answered as honestly as she could. She told Sheila Moran, "I can't imagine my life changing. The things I'm interested in are things money can't buy." But she said she might purchase a harpsichord.

Julie heard Bob say to a television reporter, "It's great to be part of an experience when someone like Julie Roy can be judged by her peers and have justice done."

Loren said he felt the women's liberation movement and other national women's organizations should have come forward and supported the case. As the trial ended, a representative of the National Organization of Women had rushed up to him and said, "We want to help you," and Loren had demanded, "Where were you when we needed you?"

That night there was a victory party at Bob's apartment. Telegrams poured in; the phone rang and rang. As Julie watched the guests celebrating, she thought, I don't consider this a personal triumph, I did only what I had to do. While listening to Mr. Halpern and Dr. Hartogs depict her as "this lesbian" and "this drunk," she felt detached because the real humiliation was long gone—the worthlessness she had felt during and after her nineteen months of what Dr. Hartogs called therapy.

If there hadn't been a trial, she was pretty sure she would be dead. At one time she had been very serious about killing Dr. Hartogs, then herself. Perhaps she would have done so if there had not been the lawsuit and Bob and Loren's belief in her. Their support had been part of her survival for four years; with their help, she had regained some respect for herself.

In the days following the trial she felt that the courtroom proceedings had been cleansing in a therapeutic sense. Having heard Dr. Gaylin, Dr. Schneck, Dr. Salzman, Dr. Anderson, and Dr. Dahlberg testify on her behalf, she now had a different feeling about psychiatrists. After the verdict Dr. Dahlberg offered to see her at no charge because he thought she would feel guilty and need to discuss her feelings. Loren and Bob persuaded her to accept his generous offer, and while with him she brought up the possibility Dr. Hartogs might kill himself. Dr. Dahlberg did not believe this likely.

She felt a certain sadness for Dr. Hartogs, for he had destroyed his own reputation. Yet she was furious at the thought that he would continue to practice. Many therapists would refuse to refer patients to him as a result of the trial, but numerous troubled men, women, and adolescents would still reach Dr. Hartogs by accident or by referral from others who were not aware of his unethical behavior.

She wondered why, of all the women Dr. Hartogs seduced under the guise of therapy, she had been the one to bring the suit. She saw herself now, as always, having been desperate for love. As a child she had felt no one loved her, certainly not her absent father. When she grew up she did almost anything to feel loved, even for an evening, as her occasional one-night stands proved. But she knew these were desperate acts and had tried to get help from a man who was unable to help her, who himself was beset by too many conflicts.

She realized her experience with Dr. Hartogs had reawakened the feelings she had suffered when her father had abandoned her. Perhaps the trial did bring a certain feeling of revenge, she thought, a revenge she really wanted to inflict on the most important man in her life —her father.

14

Back in San Francisco, she resumed her quiet life. Loren wrote her that the suit and its decision had indeed made legal history—in the nation, perhaps the world. She had won a landmark case.

The trial was reported nationally by the Associated Press and in *Time. Barron's,* the national business and financial weekly published by Dow Jones, gave the story a front-page headline, "Malpractice Epidemic." The article stated that "while few malpractice suits have received as much publicity as *Roy* v. *Hartogs,* their number has multiplied rapidly in the past few years," and that as a result, several insurance companies were withdrawing from the field of malpractice insurance.

She learned that within six months after the trial, premium rates for medical malpractice insurance in New York State increased 20 percent. In New Jersey, rates went up 49.5 percent. Around the country psychiatrists, who were previously thought to be immune from malpractice suits, found themselves facing dramatic increases in rates.

Julie wondered what effect her case would have on psychiatric malpractice—whether it would inspire more women to bring charges that were justified or stir to action some women who only had fantasies of being seduced by therapists.

Loren told her he and Bob had received a letter from

261

another attorney who congratulated them on their work in the case and concluded, "My hope is that others like [Dr. Hartogs] will thereby be dissuaded from molesting the children we all become in psychotherapy."

It was a blow to learn that on July 2, 1975, Judge Myers had reduced by $200,000 the jury's compensatory verdict, leaving only $50,000 for damages in that category, but allowing the $100,000 in punitive damages to stand. The judge said the plaintiff had not proved that "permanent emotional damage" resulted from Dr. Hartogs' "treatment."

In a twenty-three-page opinion, Judge Myers wrote:

The court has observed this plaintiff during the trial, which lasted almost two weeks. She certainly did not appear to be psychotic. She was well poised and well groomed. She spoke coherently and related her case with precision, clarity, excellent memory, and without inhibition.

I could not discern the slightest sign of abnormal behavior during the entire trial even under what must have been harrowing cross-examination.

At the same time Judge Myers described Dr. Hartogs' behavior as "heinous and atrocious." He stated: "When one considers how vital it is both for society at large and, more particularly, for the medical profession that such conduct, as presented here, be eradicated . . . it cannot be held as a matter of law that the jury's assessment of $100,000 was excessive." He concluded, "A patient must not be fair game for a lecherous doctor."

Dr. Hartogs appealed Judge Myers' decision and later, in September 1975, filed for bankruptcy. Julie thought he might believe this action would discourage similar suit by any of his other female patients.

On January 30, 1976, the Appellate Term of the Supreme Court of New York upheld the original jury verdict that malpractice had been committed, but it cut compensatory damages to $25,000 and eliminated the punitive damages. However, because of a previous agreement, Dr. Hartogs' insurance company would pay compensatory damages in the amount of $50,000.

Bob and Loren assured her that even though the amount of damages had been reduced, her case remained a landmark. For the first time the courts had established that it was malpractice for a therapist to induce a patient to have sex with him as part of treatment.

As yet she had received not one cent of the award. But she felt money was the lesser part of the triumph. She had won the greatest victory of all, a victory no higher court could ever take away from her: Judge and jury had believed her.